Margaret Sutherland!

The Thinking Child

Brain-based learning for the foundation stage

Some men see things as they are and ask why.
Others dream things that never were and ask why not.

George Bernard Shaw

The Thinking Child

Brain-based learning for the foundation stage

Nicola Call

with Sally Featherstone

Published by Network Educational Press Ltd
PO Box 635
Stafford
ST16 1BF

First published 2003
© Nicola Call 2003

ISBN 1 85539 121 X

Project Manager: Martha Harrison
Design & layout: Neil Hawkins, NEP
Illustrations: Kerry Ingham
Front cover illustration: Annabel Spenceley

Printed in Great Britain by
MPG Books Ltd, Bodmin, Cornwall

Preface

The Thinking Child is organized according to the principles of brain-based learning. It is divided into an Introduction and then Parts One to Four, which are divided into shorter chapters. Each of these parts is prefaced with a Big Picture, which gives an overview of the contents, and ends with a 'plenary', which suggests some points for reflection.

For the sake of simplification, children are referred to throughout the book as 'he' or 'she', and practitioners as 'she', except where a specific example is being given.

Acknowledgements

Thank you to the many practitioners who so generously shared their ideas and creativity. Writing this book has been a great learning experience for me, and I am extremely grateful to Sally Featherstone for her enthusiasm and commitment to the project. Thanks are also due to Sharon James, Sheila Goode, Heather Anderson, Pat Alsopp, Jenny Barrett, Jill Koops, Kate Barnes and Siobhan Burrows. The children from Braunstone Frith Infant School in Leicester contributed by providing photographs and information about mind mapping. The reception class from Seer Green Church of England Combined School in Buckinghamshire contributed ideas and many of the children's quotations. The early years staff at Town Farm Primary School in Middlesex provided inspiration and many practical ideas. Iris Birks was kind enough to share the details of the 'Sandwell satchel'. The staff and parents of Cadbury Heath Primary School provided a case study on their SPECS project.

Above all, thank you to my husband, Josef, for giving the support that enables me to combine writing with being a mother. Thank you to my daughter, Alysia, for giving me continual first-hand experience of the needs of a pre-school child, and to Rebecca, for waiting for me to finish this book before making her entry into this world. My children are my greatest teachers: may they live and learn in a world of positive experiences, and may all their dreams be realized.

Contents

Understanding the child's brain

In this section you will:

1. Read the answers to some frequently asked questions about brain-based learning;

2. Visit a pre-school, a nursery class and a reception class where the practitioners work using brain-based learning techniques;

3. Meet four young children in these three settings, who will become quite familiar to you as you read through the book.

Step 1: Answering some frequently asked questions

What exactly is 'brain-based learning'?

'Brain-based learning' is a term used to describe how to apply theories about the brain to help children to maximize their potential for learning. Once you understand the theory behind brain-based learning, you can put its various aspects into practice and enhance the learning of the children in your care.

Is this a scheme that means that I have to start to work more formally with the children in my setting?

Absolutely not! Brain-based learning is not a scheme or a curriculum. It is a method of working that derives from an understanding of the current research into how the brain develops. We know that young children learn best through play, and the techniques that are described in this book should be incorporated into the work done on the foundation stage curriculum.

Will I need additional resources to implement brain-based learning in my setting?

You should not need to make any major purchases to implement the techniques that are described in this book. Most of your work will simply involve being creative with the resources that are already available.

Will implementing these techniques increase my workload?

Using these techniques will probably involve different work, but not necessarily more work. Brain-based learning is simply a more informed way of teaching. In fact, because you will be enhancing the learning of the children in your setting, the same time commitment should lead to far greater productivity.

If I implement brain-based learning, will it necessitate major changes of policy within my setting?

Implementing the techniques in this book should not necessitate any additional paperwork or radical alteration of current policies. Practitioners find that once they gain a better understanding of the brain and how it works, they may need to reconsider and improve upon some of their ways of working, but this does not necessitate major policy changes in most cases.

How do brain-based learning techniques fit in with the literacy and numeracy strategies?

Different practitioners implement the literacy and numeracy strategies according to their individual situations. In Part Two we discuss how to structure the more formal sessions, but brain-based principles, such as using movement, music, and visual, auditory and kinesthetic learning, apply equally to the formal and less formal sessions.

Is brain-based learning just the latest fad for education?

Brain-based learning is not a 'fad'. If the practitioner understands how the brain learns, then her teaching will be more informed and more effective. In this book you will find descriptions of the current research into how the brain functions, along with suggestions of techniques that will help to maximize children's learning. It is simply not possible to learn in a way that is not brain-based!

Step 2: Let's meet a brain

To have a good brain, first you have to exercise and then you must eat lots of apples.

Owen, aged five

In this chapter we are going to meet a human brain and learn a little about how it works. In other words, we're going to get the hard bit over first – but don't let this put you off! The intent is simply to provide a very basic overview of the major components of the human brain. Later, we will use this information as a reference point, allowing us to more easily visualize what is happening inside the minds of children as they undergo the enriching, brain-based learning experiences described in this book.

When it comes to building the human brain, nature supplies the construction materials and nurture serves as the architect that puts them together.

Ronald Kotulak[1]

Over the years, experts have developed numerous theories about the nature of intelligence and its relationship with two powerful and sometimes conflicting forces: nurture and nature. Recently, researchers have made more progress than ever before, and the mysteries of intelligence have begun to unravel. For instance, scientists have recently managed to count the numbers of brain cells within specific areas of the brain and can calculate the phenomenal number of interconnections that are made as these cells communicate with one another. Scientists now have technology that allows them to look deep inside the living, functioning brain and observe electro-chemical activity as thoughts and emotions are developed and processed. As the mysteries of the brain are unravelling, many long-held theories are being disproved and new ones developed.

What is becoming increasingly clear is that the first few years of life are the most critical in terms of physical brain development. The most significant period for the wiring of the brain is during these years. Typically, this process is nearly complete by the age of 12. We now know that there are various windows of opportunity for learning between birth and the age of three or four, but that nature gives a child's brain a second chance between the ages of about four and 12. This means that an enormous responsibility lies in the hands of parents and early years practitioners.

At the micro level, the human brain consists of about one hundred billion nerve cells, called *neurons*. These neurons can be thought of as very simple data processors, which work together to solve a particular problem as it is presented to the brain. The human brain is able to easily perform tasks that the largest, most expensive computers today find impossible to accomplish. Some everyday examples of these tasks include understanding spoken human language, identifying objects by sight, sound, smell, touch and taste, and writing and understanding literature. Whereas computer processors typically attack problems sequentially, one piece at a time, the power of the human brain lies in its ability to orchestrate the activities of billions of individual neurons working together. Thus, the human brain can be likened to a symphony conductor.

Neurons develop *dendrites* for transmitting information to other neurons and *axons* for receiving information. As patterns of thought are first initiated and subsequently repeated, the participating neurons continually process and communicate. In doing so, they build stronger and more direct dendrite-to-axon pathways, called *synapses*, to other neurons. In other words, with repeated stimulation, these connections become even stronger and more established, and the brain has in effect 'learned' how to solve that particular problem. At this point, the brain is ready to undertake further learning. Interestingly, those neurons that do not generate synapses quite literally die off.

At the macro level, the brain can be thought of in three parts: the *brain stem*, the *limbic system* and the *cerebral cortex*. These parts of the brain are divided again into specific areas, each with an individual and complex role to play. Some areas process information gleaned from the senses, while others process different aspects of our emotional responses. Some are responsible for laying down certain types of memory, while others help us to 'read' cues from other people and make appropriate emotional and physical responses.

The brain stem is physically the lower part of the brain, which connects to the spinal cord. The brain stem and cerebellum are often referred to as 'the reptilian brain'. This part of the brain is primarily responsible for the body's survival systems: for regulating our life support mechanisms such as heart rate and breathing, and for what is known as the 'flight or fight' response to perceived danger. Under stress, our basic survival instincts kick in and we produce chemicals that put the body under heightened alert. During these times of stress, higher order thinking becomes derailed, and learning cannot take place effectively. It is for this reason that ideal learning environments are those that reduce a child's stress level to its absolute minimum.

CEREBRAL CORTEX *(thinking brain)*

Corpus Callosum

LIMBIC SYSTEM *(mid-brain)*

Hippocampus

CEREBELLUM

BRAIN STEM *(reptilian brain)*

Between the brain stem and the cerebral cortex is the limbic system. This is sometimes referred to as 'the mid-brain'. The limbic system consists of several structures that manage our emotions and are responsible for some aspects of memory. The lower structures of the limbic system control our more basic emotional responses, while the higher ones are responsible for making a more intellectual response. For example, if you were to hear an unfair criticism of your work, the lower areas of the limbic system would deal with your more spontaneous responses such as blushing or shaking, while the higher areas would process the social issues that might help you to make a measured response to your critic. This makes sense, as the higher parts of the limbic system are in closer contact with the cerebral cortex, where the most sophisticated thought processes take place.

The cerebral cortex is the largest part of the brain. It is sometimes referred to as 'the thinking brain'. The cerebral cortex is physically separated into two hemispheres, rather like two halves of a walnut. Scientists are constantly discovering more about the left-right relationship. Communication between the two hemispheres is needed for even simple tasks to be undertaken. For example, when listening to a piece of music, the left hemisphere is responsible for identifying the tune, analysing and recognizing sequences and rhythms, and identifying changes in volume. Meanwhile, the right hemisphere works on the 'bigger picture', while making pitch judgements and distinguishing between timbres.[2] For effective learning, the hemispheres need to each do their own job and communicate effectively. The task of providing for and managing this inter-hemisphere communication belongs to the *corpus callosum*, which is like a super-highway through which messages travel.

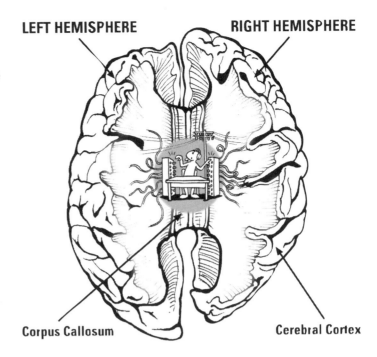

LEFT HEMISPHERE

RIGHT HEMISPHERE

Corpus Callosum

Cerebral Cortex

Throughout this book you will find references to various parts of the brain along with explanations of research that supports the theory behind brain-based learning techniques. What is perhaps startling is the fact that altering a child's environment and breadth of experiences can actually make a radical difference to his or her IQ level at a later age:

 Within a broad range set by one's genes, there is now increasing understanding that the environment can affect where you are within that range. You can't make a 70 IQ person into a 120 IQ person, but you can change their IQ measure in different ways, perhaps as much as 20 points up or down, based on their environment.

Ronald Kotulak[3]

As we become more informed about the functioning and capability of the brain, we can become increasingly effective in helping children to learn. Scientists are helping to inform our practice more now than ever before. It is an exciting time to be involved with the learning of young children, and the adventure is only just beginning.

Step 3: Meeting the children in their settings

 We teachers can only help the work going on, as servants wait upon a master.

Maria Montessori[4]

Today we are going to spend some time in an early years setting where the staff have been using brain-based learning techniques for several years. This setting consists of a pre-school situated in the church hall, and a nursery and reception class in the school next door. The practitioners here enjoy a strong relationship and work to ensure good continuity and progression. We will meet four children: George, who attends the pre-school; Carrie, who is the oldest child in the nursery; and Kishan and Samantha, who are both in the full-time reception class.

These four children are not 'case studies'. They are fictitious characters who are used throughout the text to illustrate how learning is affected by the choices made by adults around them. Although our focus is on the foundation stage, at times we will draw upon research into very early child development, including foetal development. This is because we often need to understand the significance of what has gone before in order to make sense of where the child currently 'is'. What happens in the earliest weeks, months and years will shape the brains of the children who enter our settings.

Our first stop is at the church hall, where the pre-school session is just beginning. A practitioner greets each child by name. The children are encouraged to take off their coats and organize their bags independently into labelled boxes at the door. The atmosphere is calm and serene, in part due to the quiet strains of Beethoven playing on the CD player at the back of the hall.

Children then go with their parents to look at the weekly planner and today's To Do list on the free-standing whiteboard. The children are being given the Big Picture as they read that this week they are going to investigate sponges. There are sponges everywhere: giant sponges in the water tray, triangular sponges in the painting trays and big yellow sponges in buckets next to a sign that reads 'car wash'. The parents settle their children to activities before saying goodbye. Two parents are staying to help for the morning. George's mother also stays for a while. She settles down to read a few stories with a group of children.

Let's meet George

George is one of the youngest in the pre-school, which he attends three mornings per week. He is glad that his mother is staying for a while this morning, as it has taken him some time to settle into the pre-school routine. To look at George, you would not realize that he is one of the youngest children in the room. At just one ounce less than 10lbs at birth, George has always been large for his age. His father is pleased that George was a larger baby, because he has read recent claims that bigger babies are more intelligent!

In August 2001, the *British Medical Journal* published details of a study that showed that there is a link between birth weight and IQ, even when factors such as the family's socio-economic background are taken into account. The researchers found that those who weighed more than the average of 5.5lbs did better on intelligence tests than those who weighed less.[5]

The pre-school leader also read accounts of this research, but she didn't create a new column in her record book to record each child's birth weight! For her, the most interesting point was that the study showed that there seemed to be a vital point at about the age of eight, where the child's test scores had the greatest significance regarding his future attainment. This brought home to her the enormous responsibility of early years educators.

George is the only child in his family and he receives considerable attention from his extended family. This will most likely mean that George's brain is larger than that of a child who has only experienced an impoverished environment.

In the nineteenth century, Charles Darwin conducted research on the brain sizes of domestic rabbits versus those who lived in the wild:

 I have shewn that the brains of domestic rabbits are considerably reduced in bulk, in comparison with those of the wild rabbit or hare; and this may be attributed to their having been closely confined during many generations, so that they have exerted their intellect, instincts, senses and voluntary movements but little.

Charles Darwin[6]

Since Darwin's time, researchers have confirmed his findings by showing that laboratory animals kept in enriched environments grow a thicker cerebral cortex than animals kept in impoverished surroundings. If a child is brought up in an impoverished environment, his brain suffers. From the earliest age, even before birth, exposure to positive interactions begins to establish the neural circuitry in the brain for future success.

After birth the billions of neurons begin to communicate with one another to form the complex 'wiring' of the brain. These synapses form at the astounding rate of approximately three billion per second, meaning that, by the time George was eight months old, his brain had formed about one thousand trillion connections. When a child is exploring his world and is curious, his brain cells generate numerous connectors, which sprout like tiny tree branches. Brain cells that are not stimulated soon die. It truly is a case of 'use it or lose it'.

Thankfully, George does not suffer from any lack of stimulation, and his brain is still developing at an astounding rate. But George did suffer as a newborn baby from colic. His grandmother spent time each day giving him infant massage. She didn't realize that she was also helping his physical growth and his brain development.

It has been found that children who are rarely touched are physically smaller than their peers. American researchers Schanberg and Field studied the effect that touch has on premature babies. They found that if the babies were held and their backs were rubbed, their levels of stress hormones decreased and their growth rate doubled.[7] Tactile experience also affects brain development. Experiments with monkeys have shown that repeated touching of the fingers produces a larger corresponding area in the cerebral cortex.

Furthermore, tactile experience affects emotional development. In the United States, Dr William Sears[8] has spearheaded a campaign for greater awareness of the importance of touch for children. His style of parenting has become known as 'attachment parenting'. Other experts such as Steve Biddulph comment on this difference between our culture and what he calls 'wiser cultures':

Notice how babies from many of the wiser cultures are carried around in slings and carrybags? One Balinese tradition is the first 'setting down to earth' of a new baby – it does not take place until the child is six months old. Before this it is never out of somebody's arms![9]

A baby that is carried in this way is automatically stimulated by the activity and conversation of the adult, so promoting his language and social development. Moreover, he is assured of enough touching to fully stimulate his developing nervous system. George has obviously benefited from the physical reassurance and attention that he receives at home. He is a quiet, gentle and tactile child. He is somewhat wary of new situations and often wants to follow the lead of other children, but his key-worker reassures his parents that this is quite common for summer-born children. After all, some of the other children have had almost a year's headstart on George! George clambers onto his key-worker's lap when his mother leaves. Fortunately the pre-school staff welcome physical touch from the children and George is always assured of a warm reception.

We leave the pre-school for now, and cross the playground into the main school building, where we are going to visit the nursery class. As we are about to enter the room, we see two of the nursery children on their way to the office with the register. They are holding hands and are looking up at the pictures of animals along the corridor walls. They almost collide with the returning pair from reception class, who are looking for red triangles on the ceiling.

We go into the nursery, where the children are busy with their Brain Gym®[10], as they get ready for assembly. Their teacher chooses not to ask these young children to make a formal line. Instead, they have been taught to make their way to the door in a calm manner. This is where we meet Carrie, who is drawing a large letter 'C' in the air.

Let's meet Carrie

Carrie's mother calculated that she was due to be born on 31st August but Carrie did not arrive until September. This means that she is one of the oldest children in her year group. Research into the advantages and disadvantages for the oldest versus the youngest in the class tends to be contradictory. Summer-born children often seem to make as much progress as their older peers over a year, but it is important to take their 'starting point' into account. This is now being recognized in the UK, with measures being considered such as additional support for the younger children and the adaptation of the curriculum, assessments and test scores.

Because Carrie was born late, she was not a 'summer-born' child after all. Her birth was straightforward and she had an Apgar score of nine when tested one minute after her arrival. Although parents are always relieved when their baby receives a healthy Apgar score, it is in no way a baby IQ test. Yet it is astounding to reflect on the fact that, at birth, a baby has about one hundred billion brain cells or neurons. Until recently it was believed that after birth the human brain was incapable of manufacturing more neurons. We now know that this is wrong.

Fascinating Fact

Dr. Virginia Apgar devised the Apgar score in 1952. Newborn babies are assessed immediately after birth for skin colour, muscle tone, heart rate, reflexes and respiration, and given a score of 0, 1 or 2 for each.

Scientists at the Salk Institute in California have proved that mature people do create additional neurons in a section of the *hippocampus*.[11] This finding has excited researchers with its potential for treating disorders involving neuron damage.

Carrie's one hundred billion brain cells had been produced at the staggering rate of over four thousand per second, if averaged out for her nine months in the womb. But this was the last thing on her mother's mind as, within moments of birth, she held her to her breast. Carrie's mother was convinced of the health benefits of breastfeeding, but had not realized that scientists have now proved that breastfeeding increases a child's IQ, or perhaps more accurately, that bottle-feeding can potentially lower a child's IQ. In a study in 1999, researchers at the University of Kentucky found that even after breaking out socio-economic factors, breastfed babies scored higher in IQ tests than formula-fed infants.[12]

Fats are an important component of the brain cell membrane and the myelin sheath around each nerve, and breast milk provides the exact types and proportions of fats such as the fatty acid DHA to maximize an infant's brain development. In her first year Carrie's brain tripled in size, and during this stage of rapid central nervous system growth, her brain used 60 per cent of the total energy that she consumed.

Carrie's mother still takes care to monitor her daughter's diet and to limit the amount of artificial food additives that Carrie consumes. Carrie attends a breakfast club because her mother, who is a single parent, has to commute several miles to work. The children at breakfast club are fed a healthy balanced meal. The teachers also provide healthy snacks and drinks during the day, realizing that young children perform better when allowed to eat little and often and when they are fully hydrated. As Carrie joins hands with her friend ready to make her way to assembly, we move on to visit the reception class next door.

The reception class entered school earlier to the lively sound of Bill Haley's *Greatest Hits*. The teacher welcomed each child by using his name and giving him eye contact. If she was drawn into conversation by a parent, she used the child's name soon afterwards. This is a school policy. The teacher also recalls small details of children's lives – details that might seem insignificant to an adult, but can be major for the child. As we walk into the room, she is asking Samantha about her dental appointment last Friday.

Once the children have said goodbye to their parents, the teacher changes the music to a CD of relaxing ocean sounds. For the few minutes before assembly, the children start practising writing their names in the air with their hands. Some write the initial letters, while others write their full name. A few use home-made 'magic wands'. The children write in the air with their eyes closed, using right hand, then left hand, then using both hands. Soon it is time to line up.

The children listen carefully to the teacher. 'Those of you with long brown hair can line up first' she says, slowly and deliberately. 'That's almost right, Jake, you do have brown hair. But is it long or is it short?' Jake sits back down. 'Now those with short brown hair may line up,' she continues, and Jake joins the line.

Reception class arrive at assembly, having counted ten red triangles and eight blue squares on the corridor ceiling on their way. The children who are seated in the hall are not bored; there is plenty to look at while they wait. The practitioners encourage the children to 'dance' to music with their hands in the air or to look at a Monet print at the front of the hall. There is no static display in this school; there are always new things to stimulate children's thinking. Before assembly ends, there is the sound of applause as the achievements of individuals and groups are recognized. Music is then heard again through the corridors, and the children leave quietly.

Back in the classroom, the reception children begin their literacy session. Some of them will complete a whole hour of structured activities, whereas others will move onto other activities before the end of the session. The children listen to the teacher giving the Big Picture. When she has finished her explanation, she asks if every child is 'on a green light'. A few are still 'on amber' so she repeats the explanation until everyone is confident that they understand. In this session, the children at one table are working on green sheets of paper. 'Green is for go go go!' a little girl says to the child sitting next to her.

Groups of children are working in different areas of the classroom. In fact, an observer may describe what many of them are doing as 'play'. That is because their teacher recognizes that play for young children is indeed work. One group, wearing hairnets, are cooking plastic vegetables and writing recipes in the home corner. Five or six others are touring the room with clipboards, deeply involved in an imaginary game that involves collecting red items, drawing them and taking notes. One of these children goes into the home corner, where he holds a deep conversation with the hairnetted cooks about how to spell 'red pepper'.

The groups of children concentrate well for five or six minutes, when it is time for the teacher to help some of them to refocus. Whenever there is a drop in concentration or a child starts to go offtask, *The Three A's* system of *Acknowledgement, Approval* and *Affirmation* is used. Some of the children are now ready for their first brain break.

The Three A's are **Acknowledgement, Approval** and **Affirmation**, and are discussed in depth on pages 51–55.

The classroom assistant leads the children in the 'cross crawl' exercise. Children will take regular brain breaks throughout the session, often coinciding with beginning a new type of activity.

Towards the end of this session we meet Kishan, who is pouring himself a glass of water. He then settles back down to his task. After another ten minutes, he goes to the mat to demonstrate 'good listening' before his teacher sends the class out to play.

Let's meet Kishan

If you ask Kishan how old he is, he will tell you, 'I'm almost five-and-three-quarters'. He has been in reception class for two terms. Kishan didn't attend either the pre-school or the nursery class, because he was settled at the full-time day care centre that he attended from the age of three months.

Kishan's family is bilingual. His parents are the first generation of their families to be born in the United Kingdom, and speak Bengali and English fluently. Like countless others, Kishan will become fluent and fully literate in both languages with little difficulty. Research indicates that bilingual children attain higher scores on some IQ measurements than their peers and that exposure to a different language promotes higher-order thinking. In 1962, a study by Elizabeth Peal and Wallace Lambert of McGill University in Canada[13] found that bilingual children showed significant improvements in their cognitive performance:

Bilingual children, relative to monolingual controls, displayed greater cognitive flexibility, creativity and divergent thought.

It is essential that babies hear the phonemes of any language that their parents wish them to speak while they are very young. Children's ability to learn multiple languages at a very early age is incredible. But if they have not heard the phonemes of a language by six months, their ability to identify the unfamiliar sounds diminishes fast, for example between the letters 'l' and 'r'. Children need to be exposed very early to the maximum amount of language if their ability to learn is to be fully exploited.

Any impairment to hearing may significantly impact a child's language development. Children with hearing loss are often more impulsive than their peers, and can tend to be more physical and even aggressive. Kishan's behaviour can sometimes be described as rambunctious and even challenging. Because he is a boy, he is at least three times as likely as the girls in his class to be diagnosed as having behaviour difficulties such as ADHD. His teacher is working to help him to manage his impulsivity. In her opinion, Kishan's behaviour is normal for a child with a highly inquisitive nature and boundless energy!

ADHD = Attention Deficit and Hyperactivity Disorder. We discuss ADHD on page 70.

Fortunately, Kishan's teacher sees his energetic nature as a positive trait. She uses *The Three A's* motivational system to help her to manage Kishan's boisterous behaviour. Kishan's brain probably has a proportionately larger right hemisphere than Carrie's or Samantha's. This possibly contributes to his strengths in activities that involve manipulating objects through three dimensions and spatial awareness. Out in the play area, he has taken charge of a mixed group of children as they build a dinosaur from some big cardboard boxes. Other children ride bikes, while others play in the sand and water trays. Another group of children are in dressing-up clothes and are using a

wooden platform as a stage for their game of *The Three Bears.* The play area is full of activity, with a supply of equipment for physical and imaginative play. There is plenty for everyone, and the teacher suggests, directs and organizes games for those who do not do so independently. She participates and communicates with the children, recognizing and praising good social skills.

The reception children go back into the classroom and sit down for their snack. The teacher points to a poster on the wall as she reminds them of the rules for 'good sitting' as the fruit is handed out. They then move on to maths. They start by doing 'body maths'. Alongside verbal instructions, the teacher uses visual cues. Today she shows cards with bold pictures of different shapes. The children are asked to represent each shape with their bodies, first individually and then in groups. As we leave the reception classroom to go back to see what is happening in the nursery, we can hear the teacher saying, 'That's a very accurate square, Kishan. Now, can you turn it into a triangle?'

Meanwhile, over in the nursery, the children are making a giant mind map about 'water' on the carpet. The word 'water' is printed in bold letters on a card in the centre of the map, and the children are working to organize pictures and related objects around it. These are joined with strips of card that indicate the relationship between concepts, such as a toy watering can being linked with a strip of card to a picture of a tap. Sponges feature in two places on this hands-on map; near the words 'bath' and 'washing up'. The teacher throws a new word into the discussion: 'absorb'. A round of applause celebrates the group's success as the mind map is complete for today.

The nursery children then move away to take part in different activities. Before they go, they tell the teacher what they plan to do next. She simply nods or gives a 'thumbs-up' to some children, but with others she asks a question or makes a suggestion about their plan. Some children put on coats and go outside. Others choose to stay indoors. Activities outdoors mirror the work going on inside. A box of hats and a reel of bus tickets have been left in a basket near the bricks. Soon a group of children start work on building a bus, while a second group organizes the sponges ready to give the bus a wash! Carrie and her friend fetch marker pens and sheets of card to make a sign for the bus stop. Very soon an elaborate game has begun. The nursery nurse watches and facilitates, while allowing the creativity and spontaneity of the children to lead the game.

When we leave the nursery and walk back to watch the pre-school group, we find that George and his friends are busy too. The pre-school shares use of the church hall with several other local groups, and everything has to be put out and packed away each day but this does not reduce the determination of the practitioners! The experiences they offer are of the highest quality they can possibly manage, and they work hard to make the setting stimulating and varied. George goes out to play in the small fenced-off garden next to the church hall before coming indoors to do some painting.

Eventually it is time for the pre-school and nursery children to tidy up and review their morning before going home, and for the reception children to wash their hands for lunch. The nursery children have built a very elaborate bus station, and reception class have completed their literacy and maths sessions, and spent some time on a variety of self-selected activities. Each group of children sits down to review their morning with an adult before writing a To Do list for the next day or session.

As the reception children go back into class after lunch we go to watch the second group of nursery children arrive. They are greeted with music that will set the mood for the afternoon. The nursery is set up similarly to the morning session, but with a few differences. The afternoon group's To Do list from last week included a wish to discover more about sharks. One of the children had brought a leaflet into school on Friday from a trip to an aquarium, and an interest had been sparked. A table is therefore laid out with books about sharks, a selection of seashells and some pieces of natural sea sponge. A fish tank has been borrowed for the afternoon. Some fine felt pens and a selection of paper are laid out nearby for children to draw pictures.

The afternoon in the nursery turns out to be very different to the morning. When the children go outside, they ignore the bus conductor's hat in the box and the bus tickets. Instead, they put on pirates hats and build a shark from the bricks – one big enough to eat Jonah! They use the sponges to cool down the shark, which has become beached on the shore. Eventually, the shark is freed into the ocean without biting anyone too severely, and the children go inside to hear the story of Jonah and the whale. There is no dead time in this classroom!

We leave the nursery and go to visit reception class, who are having a busy afternoon. They start by doing a few minutes of maths to music, singing their numbers from one to 20. The class then gets changed into PE kit and goes into the hall to use the large climbing apparatus. The teacher reinforces body awareness and maths concepts through questioning. She encourages children to use their natural inclination to talk to themselves as they use mathematical language to describe their movements. Language use is encouraged throughout the session: there is no rule of silence in the gym. The PE lesson is ended with the 'One, Two, Three' game. A few children hold numeral cards in different areas of the room. The teacher calls out a number and children have to skip, jump or hop towards the correct card. To make it trickier, the teacher then gives sums that the children have to answer before moving towards the numeral. On the way back to class and as they get dressed, again the children sing number songs and rhymes.

Once they are back into their school clothes, groups of children work on practical tasks involving lots of glue, plastic bottles, card and paint. The equipment that they need is organized so that they can work quite independently. In last week's literacy sessions, the teacher had introduced the author Richard Scarry. The class had been particularly inspired by his books about 'things that go', including vehicles that had little hope of ever going anywhere! This week the children can choose to be inventors. They put on 'Inventor' badges and set to work with a wide selection of materials including pulleys, ropes, guttering and wheels. This is where we meet Samantha, who has started to find the activity assigned to her group difficult.

Let's meet Samantha

Samantha's mother read numerous books about infant development when she was expecting Samantha. She was convinced that her baby recognized certain pieces of music and responded when they were played, and so she was not surprised to read that twenty weeks after conception, Samantha could hear in utero. Within an hour of her birth, Samantha preferred her mother's voice and would turn in response to it. Beverly Shirk, a paediatric nurse at Penn State Children's Hospital in the United States, recently studied the effects of recorded music versus the mother's voice upon sick children. Shirk and her team worked with 29 young children with critical illnesses. Either a recording of music, or one of the mother's voice with the music playing in the background, was played to each sick child. The effect on each child's level of agitation was monitored. Shirk reported that: *'The children were most sedate when we used the therapeutic music combined with the mother's voice.'*[14]

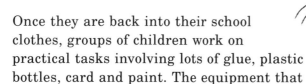

Samantha's mother frequently sang to her before and after she was born, and constantly talked to her. When she did this, she was activating the connections between the neurons that are used for language. She was stimulating Samantha's brain to develop pathways used in pitch discrimination and later in identifying patterns of sound in the phonemic stage of reading. Unlike Kishan, Samantha speaks only English at home, and her brain is already running out of time to be really good at another language. The window of opportunity for learning a second language is from birth to the age of 12.

Samantha's neural development was different to that of the other boys in her class, because she is a girl. Girls often demonstrate an early advantage with language acquisition. Samantha was a particularly early talker. By her first birthday she had a vocabulary of about 30 words and from that point onwards, her language acquisition was explosive. Her teacher recently read about the importance of encouraging children to 'pole-bridge'. Pole-bridging is when you mutter your thoughts aloud. Samantha's mother noticed that Samantha did this instinctively as a toddler, yet as she matured she became more aware of social etiquette, which doesn't encourage talking to oneself! Samantha's teacher encourages all the children to pole-bridge, and explains to their parents that this means that the child lays down even more neural connections. Connections become permanent only through regular revision, through practising the activity in the same way, practising it with some variations, and by adding language to the activity.

Turn to page 85 for more about pole-bridging.

Samantha's parents were delighted that she was offered a place at this school when they recently moved into the area. Samantha had attended a pre-school previously, where she had become confident and had made good all-round progress. She had then transferred to a nearby school where the practitioner favoured rote-learning. This type of teaching made Samantha feel anxious, which severely inhibited her learning. In situations of anxiety the body produces high levels of stress hormones. The hippocampus, which deals with memory, shuts down when the child feels stress. So at the end of a stressful lesson at that school, Samantha would remember how she felt, but not what the practitioner had intended her to learn.

Fascinating Fact

Practitioners know that children who suffer from continual stress do not find learning easy. What they probably don't know is that the brains of these children have often become physically different to those of their more relaxed peers. Research on baboons has shown that stress can actually lead to shrinkage of the hippocampus.[15]

Fortunately, the practitioners in this setting understand the importance of creating a low-stress environment in order to maximize learning. Samantha is trying to fix a wheel onto her model car. Her teacher realizes that she is not finding it easy to stay on task, so puts the model aside until tomorrow and suggests that she goes outside to experiment with a ready-built car on the ramp. The classroom assistant helps her to verbalize her observations. When Samantha returns to the classroom, her teacher asks her to record her ideas on the class mind map with her group. Other children go outside to test their inventions and to use the big pulleys that the practitioners set up there at lunchtime. A few children have chosen to leave the activity to play elsewhere.

The afternoon in reception class continues with a sense of purposeful activity until eventually it is time to tidy up. This goes smoothly because the teacher uses familiar 'tidy-up music' to signal to the children that everybody should be busy helping. She allows time to review the session and write Tuesday's To Do list, before story time. At the end of the day, children leave school clutching an assortment of books, certificates, notes and messages about their day. A number of children, including Samantha, have asked to borrow books by Richard Scarry from the book corner. They write their names on the 'Borrower's List' by the board. Celebration music can be heard from reception as the children put on their coats to go home. The nursery children leave to the sound of the song *Lifted* by Lighthouse Family. There is a relaxed atmosphere as some of the parents come into the classrooms to look at the To Do list and see their children's work.

After the children go home or to after-school club, we leave the school feeling inspired to find out more about brain-based learning. What is the theory behind the many interesting things that we saw in action today? What research is there to back up the policies that the practitioners follow so enthusiastically? How did they start on their road to using these techniques? These are some of the questions that will be addressed in this book. The answers will hopefully help you to set out with confidence using brain-based learning techniques.

Some points for reflection:

At the beginning of this chapter, you read some questions that are among the most frequently asked by practitioners who want to find out about brain-based learning. How did you feel as you read the answers? What further questions might you like to ask?

We visited an early years setting where brain-based learning techniques are used. What aspects of their work seemed similar to those in your setting? What were the key differences? What were the three things on this visit that most interested you?

What did you think when you read the description of the brains of the fictitious children George, Carrie, Kishan and Samantha? They all come from enriched environments, yet their brains are all unique. Did the descriptions make you think of the learning behaviours of any of the children in your care?

We have hopefully answered some of your questions about brain-based learning and set the scene by our description of children in settings that use these techniques.

Now we will move on to consider the physical and emotional needs that must be addressed if children are to learn effectively.

Preparing the climate and context for learning

In this section you will:

1. Read about Maslow's 'hierarchy of needs' and consider how meeting these needs affects children's learning;

2. Learn about what Daniel Goleman calls 'emotional intelligence' and discover some ways to promote emotional literacy in your setting;

3. Consider the essential tools for learning and find out some new ways to foster strong self-esteem and the 'can-do' attitude in children;

4. Think about ways to manage children's behaviour positively and learn a new system for promoting desirable behaviours, called The Three A's;

5. Read about the importance of good relationships between practitioners, parents and carers and find out about different ways that practitioners have worked with the community.

Step 1: Addressing children's physical needs

Maslow's hierarchy of needs

The psychologist Abraham Maslow (1908–1970) developed from his work with animals what he called 'a hierarchy of needs'. If you are tired and hungry, you choose to eat before going to sleep. If you are thirsty and hungry, you drink first:

you instinctively tend to your most urgent need. These needs must be met in succession in order to optimize human performance. Lower-order needs in the hierarchy have to be met before someone can advance to higher-order functioning.

These layers extend beyond physiology. Think of a pyramid with each of these needs being a layer upon which the next can be laid. Without a strong foundation, the pinnacle cannot be built. The pinnacle is 'self-actualization', which in education we often describe as 'reaching full potential'.

These are the layers of the pyramid:

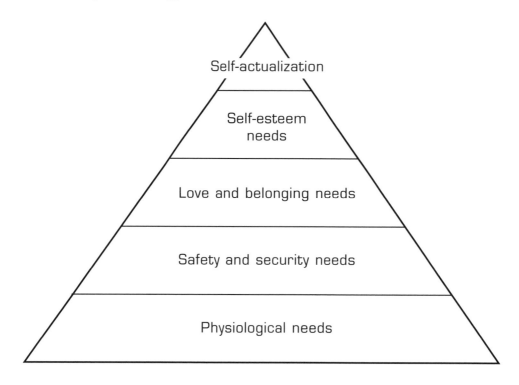

If a child is hungry, thirsty or tired, he will not be able to function. If he is worried about his safety, either at home or in the setting and feels insecure, he will not function. If he does not build strong relationships or feel a sense of belonging, he will not move onto higher-order functioning. If he has poor self-esteem, he will not believe in himself and his performance will be weak. It is our responsibility to ensure that, to the best of our ability, we provide for these hierarchical needs.

The physiological needs are the basis of the pyramid, and can be broken down into five areas: hydration, nutrition, sleep, movement and attentional systems, which we will consider in turn.

Hydration

> I like my water bottle. Grandma gave it to me. It's red and pink.
>
> Sarah, aged five

Children need to drink water throughout the day to remain hydrated, yet this basic physiological need is often ignored. Dehydration adversely affects the fluid-to-electrolyte balance in the body. For a child to be hydrated sufficiently, the equivalent of eight to 12 small glasses of water should be consumed daily, yet sometimes children go for hours without drinking during the school day.

 **Fascinating Fact**

Although the brain is only about 2.4 per cent of bodyweight it consumes up to 20 per cent of the body's energy. Enough water is needed to provide the appropriate electrolyte balance for optimal performance of the brain.

It is therefore important to ensure that water is freely available to children throughout the day. Practitioners can ensure that children remain fully hydrated by providing jugs of water for children to pour themselves drinks throughout the day, or allowing them to use refillable sports-style water bottles with sealable nozzles.

Nutrition

 A healthy country would be one where health was not dictated by accident of birth and childhood experience. Everyone should have a fair chance of a long and healthy life.

Department of Health[16]

For optimum physical and intellectual development, children need to be provided with a balanced diet. Hungry children can exhibit traits such as irritability or apathy. The chemicals that are primarily produced from food affect brain development and functioning. For example, research has highlighted the seriousness of iron deficiency on the developing brain. Iron is needed for myelination, the process by which the axons are coated with a greasy substance called myelin. Without adequate myelin, the communication between brain cells becomes sluggish. Iron deficiency in young children can lead to poor performance in problem solving and short-term memory activities.[17]

Fascinating Fact

It has been estimated that between 11 and 38 per cent of young children suffer from iron deficiency anemia in the UK.[18]

It is true that practitioners can have only a limited influence on children's diets. However, they can have influence through educating children about the importance of healthy eating, setting up breakfast clubs and timetabling regular snack times. They can also ensure that the environment in which food is served is one that is stress-free. Some of the best mealtimes are the ones where the younger children eat in their own room or a quiet area, with adults sitting at the table with them. These mealtimes also allow for the development of social and language skills.

Fascinating Fact

Chewing on gum can increase intelligence! A study has shown that chewing gum can improve mental performance. Seventy-five people were divided into three groups: one group chewed gum, one chewed imaginary gum and the third didn't chew at all. In memory tests, the chewers outperformed the non-chewers and the sham chewers.[19]

Sleep

In a study of sleep and behaviour problems among pre-schoolers, John V. Lavigne et al. described the relationship between amount of sleep and behaviour problems among pre-schoolers. Even when demographic variables were controlled, the relationship between less sleep at night and the presence of a psychiatric diagnosis was significant.[20]

George's mother was anxious to make sure that sleep was pleasant and comfortable for George. She was not willing to follow the 'cry it out' method to get him to sleep as a baby. The argument that this method 'works' was not enough to convince her that letting a baby cry himself to sleep is appropriate. We now know that the effect of long-term crying is increased levels of cortisol in the system. Cortisol is the hormone that is released during moments of stress. High levels of cortisol act as a block to normal functioning and learning, and can also negatively affect the immune system.

Researcher Christopher Coe took infant squirrel monkeys and separated them from their mothers, and then monitored their levels of 'distress calling' – that is, crying – and the cortisol levels in their blood. After a time, the monkeys ceased calling for their mothers and seemingly had overcome their distress. However, their cortisol levels remained high, and their immune systems and the development of their brains and other systems were negatively affected.[21]

Although sleep is something over which practitioners usually have little control, they can have some influence. They can plan topics about sleep and can give support to parents who are experiencing challenges with bedtime routines. They can also build in opportunities for relaxation during the day, and can vary the timetable so that the more challenging lessons are at children's most alert and receptive times.

Movement

If you are experienced, you will already know too well how energetic and physical young children are; their bodies are developing rapidly and they need to be active. It is actually painful for them at this stage of development to be still for long periods. Teaching methods should allow children to move imaginatively as well as to control and refine physical skills.

Training Support Framework for the Foundation Stage, QCA 2000

Young children are not designed to sit still for long periods. The best activities for learning are ones that require physical movement. Early years practitioners who demand that children sit for long periods to 'work' actually defeat their own aims. Getting up and moving around increases the oxygen in the bloodstream and improves concentration. In addition, adding a movement or physical action to an activity aids children who are strong kinesthetic learners – plus it adds an element of fun!

Practitioners can help children to learn most effectively by planning for activities that allow for freedom of movement. They can limit the amount of sitting still and use plenty of brain breaks. They can incorporate actions into story and circle times and use music to accompany activities. They can also monitor individual children's activities to ensure that they receive a balance of different types of play.

Attentional systems

Early years practitioners know from experience that young children do not find it easy to concentrate for lengthy periods, especially when participating in adult-directed activities. Researchers suggest that young people can concentrate for one minute for each year of their age, plus or minus one minute. Therefore five year olds need a break from any one sustained activity every four to six minutes. This may mean just an opportunity for children to reflect and refocus, or to talk about what they are doing, or to change roles within a group, or to stretch or play a short game before continuing.

Children naturally experience high and low arousal cycles during the day. At certain times, the blood flow to the brain increases and children are better at paying attention. Reception class teachers need to be mindful of the varied individual needs in their classes as they introduce the Literacy and Numeracy Strategies, and should consider how their timing impacts on the different highs and lows of attention in their class. The aim should be to sustain an optimal (not pre-determined or standard) time on task for each individual child, not to simply meet the demands of a paper curriculum.

We discuss the optimal time on task in more detail on page 78.

Practitioners can help children to learn to concentrate for longer periods by sitting and participating in activities, or organizing groups so that children with a longer concentration span play alongside the less mature children. They can also use affirmations such as, 'We are all good at reading quietly on the mat', or allow for a quiet time, or create an area where children can retreat if they feel tired.

Step 2: **Developing emotional intelligence**

What is emotional intelligence?

 There is perhaps no psychological skill more fundamental than resisting impulse. It is the root of all emotional self-control, since all emotions, by their very nature, lead to one or another impulse to act.

Daniel Goleman[22]

In his book *Emotional Intelligence: Why it Can Matter More than IQ* Daniel Goleman argues that emotional intelligence can prove to be a more significant factor in a child's future than any other measure of intelligence. Goleman quotes the research done in the 1960s by psychologist Walter Mischel at Stanford University. A group of four year olds were offered a marshmallow as a treat. If they were willing to wait for the adult to run an errand, they would be allowed two marshmallows when he returned:

Some four-year-olds were able to wait what must surely have seemed an endless 15 to 20 minutes for the experimenter to return. To sustain themselves in their struggle they covered their eyes so they wouldn't have to stare at temptation, or rested their heads in their arms, talked to themselves, sang, played games with their hands and feet, even tried to go to sleep. These plucky pre-schoolers got the two-marshmallow reward. But others, more impulsive, grabbed the one marshmallow, almost always within seconds of the experimenter's leaving the room on his 'errand'.

These four year olds were tracked down as they were graduating from high school:

The emotional and social difference between the grab-the-marshmallow pre-schoolers and their gratification-delaying peers was dramatic. Those who had resisted temptation at four were now, as adolescents, more socially competent: personally effective, self-assertive, and better able to cope with the frustrations of life.

One of the greatest challenges for the parent and practitioner is helping children to learn to manage their emotions. Indeed, impulsivity seems often to be synonymous with early years! You can help children to learn to manage impulsivity through circle time activities with a 'what if' scenario, playing games that involve waiting and turn taking, and exploring emotions and behaviour through stories, role-play and fantasy games.

Daniel Goleman identifies the five aspects of emotional literacy as:

 Self-awareness

 Management of emotions

 Self-motivation

 Handling relationships

 Empathy

Developing self-awareness and managing emotions

The key to helping children to develop self-awareness and mood management is to recognize and give labels to the emotions that they are feeling. Kishan's teacher often does this. 'You look frustrated, Kishan,' she says, when she sees him about to smash a Lego® model because he doesn't have enough pieces to make it stand upright. Kishan stops for a moment to reflect. 'I bet you're annoyed that the model keeps falling over. I would be annoyed too! Now, I wonder what we can do to get it to stand up. Who do you think might have some good ideas to help you?'

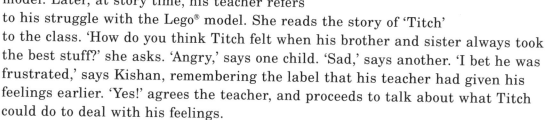

The situation for Kishan is defused. He has a label for how he felt. He is reassured that his teacher would also have felt frustrated in his situation. He absorbs the message that it's OK to feel frustrated, and that there are ways to deal with the emotion. Some of the other children give him their bricks and help him to build a base for his model. Later, at story time, his teacher refers to his struggle with the Lego® model. She reads the story of 'Titch' to the class. 'How do you think Titch felt when his brother and sister always took the best stuff?' she asks. 'Angry,' says one child. 'Sad,' says another. 'I bet he was frustrated,' says Kishan, remembering the label that his teacher had given his feelings earlier. 'Yes!' agrees the teacher, and proceeds to talk about what Titch could do to deal with his feelings.

Self-motivation

Children are born with the strong desire to learn. They do not need extrinsic motivators to persuade them to explore their world – it is instinctive to them. This intrinsic motivation usually lasts through the toddler stages into the early years.

Yet research shows that as children progress through the education system, their self-motivation declines as their dependence on extrinsic motivators increases. Sadly, in the early years this transition is sometimes already being made, as children begin to seek extrinsic rewards such as stickers or smiley faces for doing the very activities that at one time would have satisfied them. Researchers Lepper and Hodell suggest that the reason that this happens is that:

 They have met, and have been enveloped by, a system that necessarily constrains and standardizes their learning opportunities.

Lepper and Hodell [23]

Luckily for our four children, the practitioners in their settings understand that most of the children have a natural drive to learn that has not been tarnished by an emphasis on extrinsic motivators. They understand that children learn best when their curiosity is engaged, when they share ownership of what is being taught and learned, and when the level of challenge is appropriate to their individual needs.

Handling relationships and developing empathy

Research suggests that the school drop-out rate is between two and eight times higher for children with poor social skills who have not learned to read the emotional cues of others. There is also thought to be a connection between children's social skills at the age of seven and the occurrence of mental health problems in later life.[24]

Helping young children to build good relationships and develop empathy is sometimes a challenge. Some children do just seem to have better interpersonal skills than others. Howard Gardner identifies these skills as an individual 'intelligence' in his work on the multiple intelligences. An emphasis on co-operation in the setting will lead to better interpersonal skills between children. Kishan sometimes needs help with his friendships. He is always enthusiastic and finds it difficult to think through an action in preparation for an event. This can lead him into conflict with his peers.

We discuss the multiple intelligences on page 122.

Kishan's teacher encourages his enthusiasm but will step in to help him manage conflict. Sometimes Kishan needs to role-play what he plans to do, before he does it. His teacher takes the time to kneel so that she can gain strong eye contact. She draws Kishan's attention to the cues of other children and keeps her comments short and simple: 'John pushed your hand away. John didn't like you taking the brick from him.' By being explicit, his teacher is helping him to learn to read the cues of others and develop interpersonal skills.
He is developing emotional intelligence.

Step 3: Providing children with the tools for learning

Fostering strong self-esteem

 Research shows that infants' sensory experiences and social interactions with supportive adults advance their cognitive abilities.

Bornstein and Tamis-LeMonda [25]

At home Carrie continually receives positive feedback. Her mother held her for long periods as a newborn, ignoring those who said that she was spoiling her baby. Instinctively she spoke the secret language of 'motherese' to Carrie, and she encouraged Carrie to begin to explore her world with confidence.

A baby is quick to develop responses to external stimuli, and the parent plays a part in shaping this pattern of responses. Children's personality development is, in part, a reflection of what they have learned in their first three or four years. So as the child enters the early years setting, there is a personality shaped by the interactions that she has experienced so far. This could be positive, or it could be negative and inhibit the child's learning. Carrie's experiences have so far been positive. She knows that she is clever and capable, and kind and gentle. She is confident and receptive to learning.

Let us consider again Maslow's hierarchy of needs. Once a child's physiological, security and social needs are provided for, the next layer of the pyramid can be laid: that of self-esteem. Maslow divided the esteem needs again into two layers: a lower one and a higher one. At the lower level is the need for the respect of others; at the higher level is respect for oneself.

If a child feels respected by others, then the need for self-respect can be met. Yet sadly, most of us can recall one or more specific incidents in our childhood that affected our self-esteem for the worse. Thoughtless comments can affect children for a lifetime. One practitioner shared her story about how she had never learned to swim because of an experience some thirty years in her past:

One day, when I was five or six, we were having a family day at the beach. I was quite happy body-surfing in the waves, when my uncle came over and offered to take me in deeper.

Although I was a bit nervous, he took me in deeper and deeper, and then let me go when a big wave approached. I managed to surf it for a few yards, then was tossed under. I came up coughing and spluttering. It was probably only a few seconds before my uncle grabbed me, and had he given me some reassurance I would have had another go. But instead, he carried me into the shallow water and told me, 'You stay here, girl, where it's safe. I didn't realize you were too big to float.'

I never ventured out of my depth from that day onwards.

Imagine that each child in your care has pockets in his clothing which contain his self-esteem. A negative experience makes a hole in the pockets, allowing the contents to leak out, eventually leaving the child's pockets empty. After a while, the obstacles that face him on the pathway of learning might seem too daunting and his progress could be slowed or even halted. Conversely, positive experiences will help him to fill his pockets with useful attitudes and tools for his learning adventures. Positive self-esteem is one of the greatest gifts that can be given to a child. An early years setting where positive relationships are fostered ensures that children experience success. Each child then loads his or her self-esteem pockets with useful tools for learning. When a child experiences the constant respect of others, he can then develop what Maslow described as the higher level of self-esteem, which is self-respect.

Consider the difference between these two responses – both positive – by a practitioner who notices that Samantha has built an interesting model from the Duplo®:

Response 1: 'That's a great model! Well done! Can you tidy up for lunch now?'

Response 2: 'Samantha, that's an interesting model. I notice that you used just the red and blue bricks. Why did you choose those colours?'

The second response not only leads Samantha into further learning, but it also gives her some positive feedback about herself. It shows that the practitioner has really looked at the model and has thought about what she has done. It shows that her work is worthwhile and has been valued. This sort of experience helps Samantha to build strong self-esteem. The most effective practitioners aim to use only positive language in their settings. A good rule is the 'four-to-one' rule, where four pieces of positive language should be used for each neutral one.

Approval or disapproval is also exhibited through body language. Children are extremely adept at reading non-verbal cues, which can be used to boost self-esteem. A round of applause, a hug, a thumbs-up, a wink, or a pat on the back are all ways to give feedback without using words. Children can also develop their own systems for giving and receiving feedback. One reception class developed a ritual of giving each other high-fives, to a rhyme:

Five up high
Five down low,
Ten in the air
And away you go!

> Mrs Woods gives me the thumbs-up when I do good listening. I give her the thumbs-up too. It makes us laugh.
>
> Seth, aged five

You may sometimes need to make a special effort to boost the self-esteem of individual children. This might be an individual programme where all staff in the setting work to give the child explicit positive messages about himself. The activities for these children need to be planned to ensure that they experience regular success and receive support when the task is challenging, as any small event that these children perceive as 'failure' can diminish their self-esteem. Circle time is a powerful way of boosting self-esteem, and this is what we are going to consider next.

Circle time for boosting self-esteem

> Circle time is fun. My teachers sit on the floor too, but they are a bit old so they get stiff.
>
> Samir, aged four

> *Circle time provides the ideal group listening system for enhancing children's self esteem, promoting moral values, building a sense of team and developing social skills. It is a democratic system, involving all children and giving them equal rights and opportunities.*
>
> Jenny Mosley [26]

Circle time is one of the most practical tools for promoting self-esteem in young children. Each person comes to circle time with unconditional acceptance. Circle time is not a place for judgement or discipline measures. It is true that many practitioners find that discipline becomes easier and children's behaviour is seen to improve when a good circle time programme is put into place, but this is a side effect rather than an objective.

Many settings introduce circle time as soon as the children can sit in the circle for a few minutes, listen while other children speak and begin to contribute to the group. Some children are ready for this at around three years old whereas others will not be ready until later. Circle time is about sharing and reinforcing kindness, teamwork and positive attitudes; circle time reinforces positive self-images. Sessions should be short and focused.

One nursery nurse called circle time 'Sam Time', after the soft toy dog she used as a 'speaking object'. The speaking object is the object that a child holds when it is his or her turn to speak. She found that circle time was easier to manage once the children understood two simple rules. Firstly, nobody was allowed to interrupt the speaker, including herself. Secondly, children were only to say positive, kind or thoughtful things about other people. Laying down these basic principles helps circle time to go smoothly and achieve its goals.

After a warm up time, such as 'Pass on a smile', where the practitioner smiles at the first child who smiles, turns to the next child and passes the smile along, a wide variety of activities can follow. Some will actively promote positive self-esteem, for example 'Pass the speaking object', where the speaking object is passed around the circle. The children can speak when they are holding it about a topic such as 'What I did outside today', 'My best achievement this week' or 'What a friend did to help me'.

At circle time, children can revisit difficult situations and find solutions to problems. They can be given opportunities to express their feelings and develop empathy for others. Children's successes can be celebrated and their individual achievements can be recognized. They can be given opportunities to ask and answer questions within the safety of the circle, and can give and receive feedback. In these ways, circle time fosters self-esteem and emotional intelligence, which we now know are a greater indicator of future success and happiness than intellectual achievement.

The essential attitudes for effective learning

When the emotions are brought into dynamic equilibrium with reason, insight, action and even survival, learning becomes a rational, creative process.

Carla Hannaford [27]

A child will not attain the early learning goals if he does not have the attitudes that are essential for meaningful learning. These attitudes are the tools that the child loads into his self-esteem pockets and uses as he encounters challenges. Whereas skills can be directly demonstrated, taught and practised, attitudes have to be fostered. This calls for keen observation skills on the part of the practitioner. It is important to consider the attitude that the child has towards each activity. If his attitude is positive, he will be able to improve on his performance. If his attitude is negative, his performance will probably be weak and the likelihood is that next time he will repeat the poor performance rather than strive to improve and learn more.

It is as important to acknowledge the children's attitudes as it is to acknowledge their achievements. For example, when the nursery nurse in Samantha's class noticed that Samantha had sorted all the dolls' clothes according to type and size, she commented on the way that Samantha had undertaken the activity. 'Samantha, I noticed how tricky it was for you to decide what to do with the dolls' dresses. I'm impressed by the way that you stuck at the job instead of giving up – thank you!'

The child with a full set of tools for learning is:

 Enthusiastic

 Co-operative

 Confident

 Creative

 Imaginative

 Thoughtful

 Responsible

 Deliberate

 Empathetic

 Persistent

Brain-based learning for the foundation stage

Resilient

 Purposeful

 Determined

 Humorous

 Resourceful

A child with these tools has enthusiasm for all the experiences that the early years can offer. He can co-operate in a group, and contributes confidently. He may have preferences for certain types of activities, and these preferences may alter according to his needs, but he is keen to participate, and he is creative and imaginative in his play. Yet he also thinks before he acts – he has emotional intelligence and he can delay gratification and consider the possible consequences of his actions before acting. He takes responsibility for his actions and is deliberate in his thought processes.

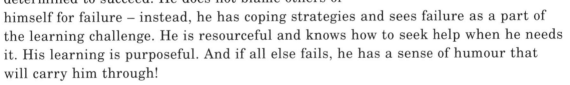

This child has empathy and can see issues from different perspectives. He is versatile and can adapt to new challenges. When faced with a challenge, he is persistent and resilient. He is determined to succeed. He does not blame others or himself for failure – instead, he has coping strategies and sees failure as a part of the learning challenge. He is resourceful and knows how to seek help when he needs it. His learning is purposeful. And if all else fails, he has a sense of humour that will carry him through!

Our four children, George, Carrie, Kishan and Samantha, have different combinations of these attributes in varying levels. It is the job of the adults who care for them to help them to build upon these. No two children are the same, and each child's profile will develop and alter according to his experiences and stage of development. When a child has a full set of these attributes, he will have a strong 'can-do' attitude, which is one of the greatest gifts that you can give the children in your care.

We can do it!
Children with strong self-esteem have what could be called a 'can-do' attitude. This 'can-do' attitude needs to be fostered in the early years, as it lays the foundations for positive learning attitudes in later life. This is equally important across all areas, from social and personal skills to physical and intellectual development. It is as important that a child believes that he can speak aloud in circle time as it is that he feels that he can dress himself, wash his hands or learn to read independently. The key to successful learning is for the child to have the skills for success along with a strong self-belief that he will succeed.

George sometimes needs adult support when he encounters a challenge. For example, when he sat to thread some beads in the maths area, he found the activity challenging. An adult sat down at the table and helped him. After a while, George discovered that if he held the beads firmly on the table, he could manage the threading independently. His self-esteem was boosted as he experienced success. If he frequently receives support in this way he will become more persistent.

In George's pre-school the adults often discuss ways to help the children become more independent. The pre-school is in shared accommodation, and everything has to be packed up after each session. In spite of this, the practitioners have made many adjustments to the room that help children to do things for themselves. The coat pegs are fixed at a lower height, so that children can hang up and fetch their own coats; boxes and shelves are clearly labelled to help children with making choices; drinks are set out on a low table, so that children can help themselves; and there is a step stool in the bathroom so that children can wash their own hands. The adults encourage children to plan their own time and to select and put away the equipment as they need it. The practitioners are also careful to ensure that they model the 'can-do' attitude themselves. For example, when a new go-cart was delivered in pieces in a big box, the practitioners gathered the tools that they needed and built the go-cart with the children. Photographs were then used to make a book about the activity.

Practitioners need to work to ensure that children also develop a 'can-do' attitude to literacy: all children should believe that they are readers and writers, no matter what their stage of literacy development. Opportunities should be given for children to write for a purpose, such as writing shopping lists, letters to Grandma, signs, labels and reminder notes. Writing materials should also be provided for children to use in role-play activities. For example, in one reception class the children helped to convert their home corner into a garden centre. They made labels and price tags, wrote out receipts for customers and put up signs about how to care for the plants.

Even from the earliest stages of mark making, it is important to encourage children to believe that they are writing. A childminder spoke of her amazement when she saw her youngest child imitate the older children when using chalks on the patio outside:

The four year olds that I look after were drawing on the patio. They would attempt to write their names near to their drawings, saying the letters aloud as they did so. Mia, who is only 18 months old, was following them, making little marks on the floor with a chalk from the box. She was muttering to herself, saying 'Mia' as she made each mark. She was acting like a writer even though her 'writing' was only tiny little dashes on the patio.

In Samantha's class, some children write pages of what might appear to be scribble, yet when they 'read' it aloud it contains elaborate sentences to make up a story. Other children have advanced further, and their writing contains a variety of symbols running from left to right on the page. Other children have advanced even further and include some letters and numbers in their writing. A few children include some c-v-c (consonant-vowel-consonant) words and their writing is demarcated into clear words and sentences. This is a normal range in any early years setting, but the point is that all the children are writers. You don't have to be able to spell to be able to write!

Similarly, you don't have to know phonics to be able to read. How many times have you heard a parent say, 'But he can't read – he just uses his memory'? This important stage of reading, where the child memorizes a favourite book and 'reads' it over and over again, needs to be actively encouraged. In addition to learning to recognize the words that he is 'reading' and how stories work, the child is learning a much more important lesson – the 'can-do' lesson that he can read!

In one classroom children worked in the book-making area, illustrating and binding their own books. A wide variety of materials was available: card, paper, scissors, glue, Sellotape, treasury tags, paper clips, hole punches, and so on. Some ready-made books were available for children to take and fill in with pictures and their own writing. Other children would organize their own paper and card and bring their completed books to the practitioner for her to bind them on the spiral binder. These home-made books were displayed in the book corner and on the table by the parents' notice board.

Another reception teacher devised a system to help the children in her class who were reluctant writers:

Several of the children in my class would frequently interrupt my classroom assistant or me to ask for spellings, or to ask one of us to scribe for them. They just didn't believe that they could write independently. So we set up systems for different types of writing.

Sometimes we use wordbooks, where they have to 'have a go' on one side of the page before asking an adult to check their attempt. Other times they can come to ask me to scribe for them, but when they have a green book, green paper or green pencils on their desk, it means, 'Green is for Go, Go Go!' They then are expected to write independently and not ask for help until they have finished the task.

Somehow this relieves the pressure for them and they are happy to have a go, meaning that the adults can work with other children. We love our 'Green is for Go' times!

A setting that is organized for the children to work independently fosters the 'can-do' attitude. Children who have the 'can-do' attitude see failure as part of life and learning. To foster a positive attitude towards challenge, show an interest when a child is facing difficulty but avoid solving his problems for him. Be matter-of-fact about failure, and analyze it without attaching emotion to it. Ask questions about it and help the child to problem solve. Maybe another child could help, or maybe the whole group could get involved. Maybe different materials need to be used or maybe it would be better to try again tomorrow when everyone has had a chance to think about possible solutions. Maybe success is going to take several days or several weeks, and interim targets need to be made to give structure to the process and a sense of progress.

The language used with children will affect their attitudes towards challenge. A useful tool is to use the phrase 'not *yet*'. The 'Traffic Light' system has a red light, but the meaning is 'I don't understand yet' rather than 'I don't understand'. When a child finds that he cannot do something, the response should be, 'I know you cannot do it yet, but you will be able to soon. How can we help you to learn to do it?'

The 'Traffic Light' is described on page 82.

With a 'can-do' attitude, the child is eager to learn, and he is able to learn about learning. He has a good selection of tools and no holes in his self-esteem pockets. He is emotionally literate. He is ready to learn.

Step 4: Managing behaviour positively

Tools for managing behaviour

 One test of the correctness of educational procedure is the happiness of the child.

Maria Montessori [28]

 I am good at tidying up and so is Frances.

Jon, aged three

Our aim in the early years is to help children to understand what constitutes appropriate behaviour and to help them to self-manage their behaviour. This self-control is a part of what constitutes emotional intelligence. We need to decide what our expectations are, making them appropriate to children's age and developmental stage. Many practitioners draw up a simple set of rules for their setting. In order to be effective, it is essential that any set of rules is drawn up with the children and not simply imposed upon them. This process helps them to understand the reasons behind the rules and makes it more likely that they will follow them.

Rules should be phrased positively. 'Put away the toys when you have finished playing with them.' is a lot more positive than 'Don't leave toys on the floor.'

Matching activities to the needs of the children against a background of a clear and agreed code of conduct will decrease the likelihood of undesirable behaviour. Doing this will foster the children's intrinsic motivation to learn, which in turn leads to their being motivated to behave appropriately. When the curriculum is appropriate and the right level of stimulation and challenge is offered, the other strategies that we have discussed in the last few chapters will become increasingly powerful. When children's physical needs are met and they have emotional intelligence, high self-esteem and a 'can-do' attitude, they will exhibit good learning behaviours.

But of course every practitioner knows that there are children who exhibit challenging and inappropriate behaviour due to factors that are outside the practitioner's control. For these children, the provision of an exciting and appropriate curriculum may not be enough, and a more direct behavioural approach needs to be taken. In these cases, a behaviour programme sometimes becomes necessary. This means that the process by which targets are going to be achieved is formally discussed and recorded, and the plan immediately becomes more likely to succeed.

The key to a successful behaviour programme is to devise good targets, which are then linked to an action plan. Good targets are SMART:

 S pecific: if a target is vague, it will not be successful. Be as specific as you can: when and where do you want this behaviour to occur? How often? With whom? In what sized group? At what times of day?

 Measurable: in order to assess whether a target is measurable, ask the question, 'How will we know that the target has been achieved?'

 A chievable: too many targets will be too difficult to implement at one time. Tackle the most important aspects of behaviour first, and move onto others later.

 R ealistic: targets need to be related to small steps, rather than lofty aims that cannot easily or quickly be achieved.

 T ime bonded: set a time within which you expect the target to have been reached. This should not be too long; with young children six or eight weeks should be a maximum.

These targets are only of value if they are shared with parents or carers and all those who work with the child, and then linked to a clear action plan. Some practitioners choose to also share the target directly with the child. For each target, details need to be given about how the target will be achieved. For example, last year, when Kishan attended a day care centre, the practitioners wanted him to be able to sit on the mat for story times without shouting out inappropriately or disturbing other children by touching or climbing across them. They drew up the target: *To be able to sit on the mat for one short story (maximum four minutes) without touching other children.*

The practitioners made the decision at this stage to focus on helping Kishan to learn to sit still and not to try to modify his inappropriate shouting out. After Kishan had achieved this target, they agreed that they would draw up a further action plan to help him to learn not to call out. They included a specific time limit to the length of time that they would expect Kishan to sit so that there was no ambiguity about their aims.

The next stage was to decide how they would help Kishan to achieve this target. Their action plan included ideas about how they would use *The Three A's* system, which we discuss in the next section, to help them to achieve the goal:

Mrs X to sit on chair by door during story time. Kishan to sit by her feet. Mrs X to use affirmation, 'Kishan is good at sitting still,' before the story begins.

If Kishan tries to move away, Mrs X to put hands on his shoulders and turn him gently back. If Kishan continues to move away, Mrs X to calmly take him to the Quiet Area to read a book of his choice, then allow him to play for the remainder of story time. If Kishan sits for the short story, Mrs X to acknowledge by give non-verbal feedback and then take him to the Quiet Area to play until story time is over.

The Thinking Child

Brain-based learning for the foundation stage

By being very specific about how a target is going to be achieved, the chances of success are raised considerably. Notice that the practitioners did not include any direct reward system in their action plan. They planned to use affirmations and acknowledgement, but decided that Kishan's target and behaviour was not challenging enough to warrant an extrinsic motivator such as a sticker chart. They wanted him to learn to modify his behaviour for its own sake. The 'reward' for Kishan of learning to sit for the story time was to be the pleasure of hearing the story itself: Kishan needed to become self-motivated to sit and listen.

Yet other children, usually due to external factors that are outside the practitioner's control, do need a method using extrinsic motivators to modify their behaviour. In these cases, the important principle is that the reward system must be used only for as long as it takes to modify the behaviour, and no longer. The child needs to learn that the appropriate behaviour brings about its own rewards, and so the practitioner needs to work hard to help the child to 'wean' from extrinsic rewards.

Mikey entered reception class halfway through the spring term. He had attended three schools previously and was now in his fourth foster home. Understandably, Mikey had little trust that the adults around him would remain consistent. He intended, it seemed, to prove that he was 'unlovable'. He refused to follow directions, often choosing to do the exact opposite of what was asked. If the children were sitting on the mat, Mikey would go to sit on a chair at the other end of the room. If they were lining up, he would hide under a desk or run to the door, pushing children out of his way as he went. He rarely settled to a task for more than a few seconds.

With the help of the educational psychologist, Mikey's teacher drew up a behaviour plan for him that targeted his most disruptive behaviours first – the ones that she thought would have the most positive impact on Mikey and the class if they were modified. It was vital that Mikey would feel immediate success so that his self-esteem could receive a much-needed boost. Mikey clearly needed an extrinsic reward system to help him break out of the habit of this disruptive behaviour.

But instead of simply making a sticker chart for Mikey 'behaving well' or 'being good', the teacher broke down her aims into small, manageable targets that Mikey would be successful in achieving. She linked the targets to a clear action plan showing how each was to be achieved. For example, Mikey was given a chair beside the mat to sit on when he didn't want to sit with the other children. The teacher put his name on it, and explained to the class that Mikey was to have the chair while he was settling in. At story times, Mikey was asked if he would rather sit on the mat or on the chair. He received a sticker or a smiley face for sitting on either. Giving children a choice in this

way usually removes the temptation for the child to refuse to comply with your wishes as he is being given the opportunity to make a decision for himself.

Each of Mikey's targets was planned in this way to ensure that he had the support available to ensure success. By the end of each day, Mikey's sticker chart would be quite full. He could then choose to take it home or display it in class, or to put it in his drawer. When a reward system such as this is needed for a young child, the child needs to be able to see tangible progress being made. It is no good having to wait until after lunch or the end of the day for a sticker: the feedback needs to be frequent and immediate. Gradually, as the child is successful and his targets are being met, new targets and an action plan can be drawn up, until the child has reached a level of self-motivation.

A simple system for giving meaningful and positive feedback that will impact learning and behaviour is called 'The Three A's'. That is where we head to next: The Three A's – Acknowledgement, Approval and Affirmation.

Acknowledgement

Acknowledgement needs to be given in order for us to know that we are on the right track. This is equally as true for children as it is for adults. Acknowledgement also adds to the 'feel-good factor' – and it makes the world go round!

If an inspector only reported on the negative aspects of your work, ignoring your positive achievements, how would you feel? What about if the feedback was positive, in spite of the fact that you knew there were some weaknesses in your work that day? Neither of these scenarios would optimize your learning. Acknowledgement of what you have achieved should help you to become more self-aware and self-critical. This is what we should be aiming for when we give feedback to the children in our care.

We should acknowledge achievements across the whole range of skills and children's development, not purely the academic achievements. Acknowledgement can be a powerful tool for encouraging appropriate social skills and behaviour. Yet it is easy to focus on the children who demand our attention. Numerous studies show that boys often demand more attention from teachers in classrooms across the school age range, both through assertive 'good' behaviour, and through challenging behaviour. For example, a study for the Scottish Council for Research in Education found that:

Contributions from boys predominate both physically and verbally during classroom interaction.[29]

Acknowledgement needs to be given to all children. It needs to be specific and direct, and should be given continually and consistently. It can be given verbally or non-verbally. The practitioner can smile, she can give a hug or a 'thumbs-up' sign, she can give a pat on the back, or a round of applause, or any number of other gestures. Along with the acknowledgement must come a clear explanation of what exactly is being acknowledged.

For example, three-year-old Martin walked to the park with his childminder several times each week. Every time they passed the fruit shop on the way, Martin would reach out and touch the fruit display. He seemed to find it impossible to resist! One day, before setting out, the childminder asked him, 'How could you stop yourself touching the fruit?' 'Put my hands in my pockets,' said Martin. As they reached the shop, she looked down at him. He whispered, 'Put hands in pockets.' He managed to walk past without touching anything. The childminder gave Martin a hug. 'Well done,' she said. 'You remembered about your hands all by yourself. You are a clever boy. I will tell your mum this evening.'

It is important to acknowledge success continuously, until it becomes an integral part of the children's lives. They can share in the acknowledgement of one another's successes, for example with a round of applause or a celebration song or a rhyme with actions. Eventually children will learn to spontaneously acknowledge achievements within the group, and can develop fun ways to give feedback. In one pre-school, the children sang this song when Thomas used the scissors successfully, to the tune of *Old MacDonald had a Farm*:

Oh, (Thomas) did it again

Eeee-i-eeee-i-oh

He's so smart he did it right

Eeee-i-eeee-i-oh

With a (snip snip) here

And a (snip snip) there

Here a (snip)

There a (snip)

Everywhere a (snip snip)

Oh (Thomas) did it again

Eeee-i-eeee-i-oh

This song was used for any achievements in the group, substituting the name and an appropriate description. Each time that a child's achievement is acknowledged it adds to his or her level of self-esteem. It is like adding another tool into the child's self-esteem pockets. With pockets full of useful tools, learning is so much more fun!

Approval

 When Mrs Wade is pleased with me she smiles and smiles. It makes her look very pretty and it makes me feel happy inside.

Pete, aged five

Once an achievement or behaviour has been acknowledged, the next stage is to show your approval. The purpose of showing approval is to give reassurance and encouragement, which will help to ensure that the behaviour is sustained and repeated. For some children, particularly those lacking in confidence, the need for you to show your approval is greater than for others. Some children may not need you to use this 'A' at all – they are motivated and confident enough to be able to respond to feedback without much 'stroking'. The extent to which you use each aspect or the whole of *The Three A's* will vary from child to child, and from situation to situation.

The timing of offering approval can be critical. If you give it too soon the child may be distracted and not retain his focus on the task; if you give it too late he may have become unsure or discouraged. A clear statement works best: 'Gillian, I am pleased to see you sharing the counters with Henry,' or, 'I like the way that you are trying hard to do your buckle up, Donald.' Statements of approval are effective when they are direct, relevant and personal, rather than non-specific words such as, 'Good work, Gillian and Henry,' or 'Good try, Donald.'

If non-specific words of praise are simply offered as a reaction to the child's efforts, a chain of events is likely to be started. Firstly, the child will feel good, for a few minutes. He might sustain his current activity or behaviour, or even be inspired to try harder. Alternatively, he might not be able to identify what exactly was pleasing to you, and so his efforts will either cease or will go off track. Either way, he will probably soon need a further assurance from you – another stroke – to reassure or encourage him. He is now in danger of becoming hooked on praise. An analogy would be the difference between offering a nourishing snack or a sugary sweet. The sweet may please for a moment, but it will not really satisfy. The child is likely to crave more. The nourishing snack, by contrast, will have a long-term positive effect on the child's growth and development.

In his book *Punished by Rewards*, Alfie Kohn argues that the excessive use of praise has a detrimental effect on self-motivation:

Praise is no more effective at building a healthy self-concept. We do not become confident about our abilities (or convinced that we are basically good people) just because someone else says nice things to us.[30]

Kohn argues that if praise is to be used, the practitioner should follow four basic rules:

 Don't praise people, only what people do.

 Make praise as specific as possible.

 Avoid phony praise.

 Avoid praise that sets up a competition.

Once the child knows that he has your approval and what it is for, you can now move onto the last of *The Three A's*, when you affirm that the success is going to be repeated.

Affirmation

Affirmations can be used to create the environment for success. Frequent affirmations of a child's best qualities and achievements will confirm in his mind that a success was not incidental and that it will be repeated. This is particularly important for children who have low self-esteem.

Affirmations to individuals tend to be more specific to the targets and aims for that child. For example, at the start of the year, George's key-worker felt that George needed to become more assertive in group situations. Whenever she noticed that he was taking a passive role, she would make the affirmation, 'George is good at explaining his ideas,' and if necessary follow up with, 'George, would you like to tell us what you think?'

Affirmations can also be used as a tool for instilling positive attitudes among groups. For example, the practitioners in one pre-school used the affirmation, 'We are all good at standing still when given the signal' when they gave a clap, then raised their hands in the air to gain the attention of the children. For several weeks, some of the children found it difficult to remember what the signal meant and would continue playing. But after a while, these continual affirmations paid off and all the children became good at stopping at the signal. As each child learns to believe each positive affirmation, she is being provided with a useful self-belief to put in her self-esteem pockets.

Some practitioners design and display affirmation posters. Pictures, photographs, cartoons and captions can be used. The posters should directly refer to the types of behaviours and attitudes that you wish to foster. Other practitioners put affirmations to music. Music is a wonderful vehicle for influencing mood and for triggering memories. Using music utilizes the natural ability of the brain to make associations and recall things more easily. One practitioner used a glockenspiel to play a simple tune as she made affirmations, such as 'We all sit beautifully on the mat.' Affirmations can be prefaced with the word 'you' if the practitioner is addressing the children, or by 'we' if the children are joining in.

The Three A's system gives a simple structure to help set expectations and guide the behaviour of young children. It ensures that there is a consistent and positive approach within the setting, and it presupposes that all children are capable of behaving appropriately. This positive attitude is one of the most powerful tools available to practitioners and is an essential part of brain-based learning techniques. But of course, parents have the greatest influence upon their child's attitudes and behaviour, and a partnership with them is essential if children are going to reach their potential. That is our next step: to consider how we can build that positive partnership approach with parents and carers.

Step 5: Fostering partnerships with parents and carers

 There is no more valuable way to widen everyone's horizons than by strengthening the link between home and school.

Joanne Hendrick[31]

 Mummy likes to come to nursery to play with me and the other children. She is good at painting and putting away the bricks.

Clara, aged four

The parent or carer will have more influence on what the child learns, how he learns, and what he believes, than any practitioner, no matter what setting he attends. Therefore, the stronger the partnership between parents, carers and practitioners becomes, the more effective the education will be for the child. The political climate in recent years has become one where legislation is seen as a viable way to enforce home-school partnerships, with the School Standards and Framework Act of 1998 stating that:

All maintained schools, city technology colleges and city colleges for the technology of the arts adopt a home-school agreement and associated parental declaration.

Yet common sense would suggest that any legislation is not going to be as effective as the grass-roots hard work of creating links and building positive relationships. Attention to simple details about the setting is essential. Often those who work in a setting can lose sight of the impression that might be given to a newcomer, and so it is important to stand back and assess the setting objectively every once in a while.

One school had a policy of recruiting a volunteer who had never been to the nursery to arrange to visit for a session. After this, the volunteer would give feedback to the staff about the experience. These volunteers would be asked to mention even seemingly minor details, such as how easy they found it to park and find the main entrance. The staff would then brainstorm ideas about how to improve their systems for welcoming visitors and giving the appropriate information and impression. An alternative way to do this is to elect a member of staff, a colleague or a friend to do this and act as an impartial observer for an hour or two. You might wish to draw up a list of questions to ask the volunteer.

Once you are sure that your setting is warm and welcoming to newcomers, you need to consider the effectiveness of your lines of communication with parents and carers. In the most successful settings there are strong formal and informal systems for communication. The informal aspect of parent–practitioner communication starts at the front door. An available, welcoming, smiling practitioner will automatically build good relationships. But a frequent challenge facing many practitioners is that there are some parents or carers who demand more of the practitioner's time at the beginning or end of the day than is practical. There is a difference between a parent quickly mentioning that her child has a sore toe and so must not take off her shoes in the sandpit, and a parent who wants to engage in a lengthy discussion about her child's language development first thing in the morning! By giving plenty of opportunities for lengthier discussions, the need for parents to engage staff during the working day is diminished. A regular schedule of parent conferences ensures that these issues can be dealt with outside of the normal working week. Wise practitioners keep their diary to hand at the start and end of each day. This way they can easily say, 'That sounds important. Why don't we make a time when we can talk comfortably?'

In addition to giving feedback at formal meetings and parent conferences, it is important to give parents regular informal updates about children's progress. These informal 'chats' serve two purposes: they give the parent important information about her child, and they help to build trust between the two adults. The key to good partnerships is that the parent really knows that the practitioner understands and cares about the child.

Another useful way to build good partnerships is to have a clear 'induction' programme for new children and families. It is worth investing time in organizing a few afternoons for children to visit, with maybe some special activities, and a gradual build-up to a time when the parents can move away for a discussion while their children play. As part of their induction schedule, some practitioners include home visits. One nursery school made a home visit to every new child before he started school. The children were really excited to be able to show off their house, pets, bedroom and toys. The only complaint that the staff had about the system was that they were so well entertained in the children's homes that they would gain weight from all the cakes and goodies that they were offered!

The most successful settings also have good systems for ensuring that there is clear communication about everyday events and activities. In some communities the parents welcome regular, lengthy newsletters that explain everything in detail. In other communities, it is more appropriate to give brief 'flyers', while having informal talks about important announcements or forthcoming events. Coffee mornings can ensure that information is made available to parents. Some practitioners use a whiteboard or large notice board to give information. Sometimes

a regular telephone call helps to maintain lines of communication, particularly with working parents. Sending home notes about achievements or certificates helps to inform parents and also boosts children's self-esteem.

In many communities, parents also appreciate the opportunity to learn more about child development and relevant parenting issues, for example from visiting speakers such as speech therapists, paediatric nurses, health visitors or midwives. One primary school set up a parents' campaign called SPECS, which stands for *Supportive Parents Enabling Children's Success*.[32] The aims of SPECS were to:

Emphasize the enormous impact parents can have on their children's learning; increase parental involvement in their children's education to impact upon pupil achievement; and to *support parents in their role as parents and as their children's first and enduring teachers.*

The most successful aspects of the campaign were events such as a parents' reading workshop, sessions with interesting speakers, an ICT (Information and Communication Technology) evening and an 'even better parents' course.

Some practitioners lend parents leaflets and books about child development, health issues and practical ideas for play activities. Many of these items are free, such as leaflets on family activities from the Basic Skills Agency. One innovative scheme by Sandwell LEA supplies each child with a 'Sandwell Satchel' at the start of the foundation stage. This backpack contains a range of equipment for physical activity, including a tape of movement songs, along with items such as a rubber quoit, a beanbag, a skipping rope and a soft ball. The authority believes that physical games and movement activities will give a far better preparation for the foundation stage than books and pencils!

Researchers Ghazvini and Readdick analysed the frequency of communication with parents in a variety of settings alongside the quality of education offered.[33] In the settings that were of higher general quality, the parents and caregivers reported higher levels of communication with the staff. The quality of the partnerships and communication between the home and the setting will depend also upon the ways that parents are involved in the everyday life of the setting. Different individuals have different things to offer the early years setting, but we should work from the fundamental belief that *everybody has something to offer.* Some parents prefer to play a low-profile role, whereas others have the time and desire to be involved in more ambitious projects.

One nursery teacher, realizing that she had a group of parents who did not seem comfortable working within the setting, asked for volunteers to help her to organize a resource box for her displays. It was difficult for her to find the time to cut out enough letters for titles on displays or to make interesting and imaginative borders for the boards. The parents took over the organization of the display resources. They met together for coffee twice a month and eventually started organizing complete displays. In this way, a group of parents who were initially not comfortable working within the setting found a way to contribute with confidence.

The end result of good communication and partnership between the home and the setting is a better provision for the child. There have been numerous research studies that show that there is a link between children's achievement and the level of collaboration between home and school. For example, there is a clear link between a good partnership between school and home and early literacy development, and family literacy programmes can strongly influence children's level of attainment.[34]

A child who knows that his parents and practitioners are working together as a team can be relaxed, confident and emotionally secure in the learning environment. When his emotional needs are taken care of in this way, he is more likely to develop the 'can-do' attitude and have strong self-esteem. With this secure foundation, he is able to focus on playing and learning and is able to reach his full potential.

Some points for reflection:

How are the physical needs of children met in your setting? What obstacles might lie in your way as you try to provide for these needs? How might you overcome these obstacles?

Are the children in your care emotionally literate? Which children seem the most emotionally literate? Which of them seem to need help to manage their emotions? How might you address emotional literacy in your setting?

Which children in your care have a good set of tools for learning? How do you provide for the development of these positive attitudes? How do you work to enhance children's self-esteem and promote a 'can-do' attitude? Could you make more use of circle time to actively promote strong self-esteem?

How positive is the behaviour management in your setting? How do you work to help children to learn to manage their behaviour? How might *The Three A's* system help you to reinforce good behaviour, manage challenging behaviour and foster high self-esteem?

How would you describe the partnerships that you have in your setting with parents and carers? What are the greatest strengths in your relationships? Are there any parents or carers who are not involved in any active partnership with staff? How might you address the needs of these parents and their children?

Part One

Once children's physiological and emotional needs are catered for, they are ready to learn. If their behaviour is managed positively and there are strong links between home and the setting, their learning will be all the more effective.

Part Two

Now we will move on to consider how to support independent learning through careful management of the environment, helping children to develop good listening and concentration skills, and ensuring that the feedback given is positive and supportive.

Supporting independent learning

In this section you will:

1. Consider how to organize your space in order to implement brain-based learning techniques, and read about ways that other practitioners have maximized the use of their environments;

2. Read about how children learn to pay attention and discover some ways to help them to improve their attention skills;

3. Consider what is appropriate when expecting children to stay 'on task' and read about some ways to help them to increase their concentration span;

4. Think about the type of language used in the setting by both adults and children, and consider how to question and give good feedback.

Step 1: Making maximum use of the environment

Organization of the learning environment

Within the acclaimed Reggio Emilia schools in Italy, careful attention is given to the look and feel of the classroom. Areas are organized for groups of various sizes to work on projects, and displays are carefully formed at both adult and child eye level. Common areas are designed to encourage interactions between children from different groups. Materials are arranged in ways that ensure that they are aesthetically pleasing, and use is made of mirrors, plants and interesting artefacts to engage and inform the learner. In fact, the environment is considered so important that it is referred to as the 'third teacher'.

> *The most effective kind of education is that the child should play among lovely things.*
>
> Plato

The practitioner needs to create a secure environment within which children can play and work. Children need space in which they can move, ideally moving freely between an outdoor area and the indoors. Materials need to be organized so that children can access them easily. Children need to be taught how to select and use

We discuss the use of outdoor space for maximising learning on page 100

materials appropriately and safely. Some practitioners play games where they set a hypothetical challenge, such as 'Go and fetch what you might need to make a model in the technology area.' The children can then go as individuals or groups to fetch whatever might be needed for this specific task. They can then return the materials to their correct places, as the practitioner talks through their actions, so adding language to the activity and rooting the experience more firmly in the children's memory.

Practitioners who use brain-based learning techniques find that there are some additional materials that they find indispensable in their work. Most of these are everyday items. Here is a list of items that you might find useful in introducing the ideas in this book:

A copy of the 'brain-based learning circle'

A board at children's eye level for displaying the To Do list

A traffic light for checking understanding

A whiteboard or pinboard for displaying the Big Picture

A cassette or CD player with a number of music cassettes or CDs

A large amount of blu-tac for sticking up posters, affirmations and mind maps

 Sets of coloured pens or chalks for brainstorming sessions

 Pieces of card and paper of various colours and sizes for mind maps

 Sets of affirmation posters

 A 'decibel clock' for showing children your expectations for the noise level

 Props for circle time activities such as hats and soft toys

 Magic wands and different types of pointers for Brain Gym® exercises

 A list or 'menu' of brain break ideas

 Lengths of ribbon and coloured pegs for displaying posters, pictures or mind maps

 Posters outlining rules and 'good sitting' and 'good listening'

In some situations it is easier to maintain an ideal environment than in others. Many practitioners have the challenge of having to share their environment. Some practical solutions for overcoming this challenge include:

 Making laminated labels for each areas of the room

 Using transparent boxes and bags for equipment

 Colour-coding boxes of equipment according to their contents

 Using boxes and trolleys with wheels

 Hanging display boards on hooks on the wall

 Using free-standing display boards

 Using boxes covered with fabric for 3D displays

 Using carpet samples to create comfortable book areas or home corners

For childminders, the environment is naturally more one of a 'home' than a classroom, yet many of the principles of classroom organization still hold true. For example, providing a pin-board for a To Do list is as important in this type of setting as in the classroom. A cosy child's book area can be created in the corner of a room or even behind a sofa, and children can be taught to select materials independently from well-organized shelves of art materials or labelled boxes of

toys. A free-standing display board can be used during the day, but stored away when children go home.

Whatever your situation, it is worth taking time periodically to re-evaluate the use of space in your setting. Sometimes it helps to do this with a colleague or friend who can give new ideas. Another way to evaluate the learning environment is to list the desirable aspects of each area. Rather than being restricted by the limitations of your current situation, be idealistic when you do this, and imagine your perfect book corner, art area or home corner. List all the desirable items down one side of the paper, and make notes about how you might achieve this down the other side. Don't worry if you cannot meet all your ideals at once – you can build on the plan as finances become available or when new ideas or opportunities emerge.

Some practitioners like to spend time reorganizing their room with the children's help. Obviously, heavy furniture has to be handled by adults, but the children can help with ideas. One reception class teacher discussed possible changes to the layout of the room with her class by drawing diagrams on a whiteboard. Another practitioner told how she found a solution to help the three year olds in her pre-school group learn to put materials back in the correct place:

I was spending twenty minutes each evening sorting out pencils, crayons, glue spreaders and so on into their correct containers and putting them on the right shelves. I went to visit our local infant school, where the reception teacher had a system for helping children to tidy properly. Each type of material was kept in a different shaped container. On each container was a drawing so that children could see what should go in each pot. She had then covered the shelves with sugar paper. She had drawn around the outline of the pot and in the centre had drawn a simple picture of the item to match the pot. It was so simple!

I altered the system a little to help my youngest children, by colour coding the pots. There was an immediate improvement in the children's independence in tidying. At tidy-up time my only problem for a few days was that every child wanted to tidy the pots, and nobody wanted to tidy up elsewhere!

A well-organized environment invites desirable learning behaviours. Sometimes even a slight alteration to the organisation of the environment can make a significant difference to learning and behaviour. For example, a newly qualified teacher described a difficulty that she had with the children running in the classroom:

One afternoon the Headteacher taught the class while I went on a course. The next day I was amazed to find that I didn't have to say, 'Don't run' to a single child! The Headteacher had simply shifted a few of the tables a foot or so in one or other direction. There were no longer any clear 'runways' from one activity to another, and the children had to walk in order to negotiate their way around the furniture. Now, the moment I have to ask children to walk in the classroom, I stand back and look at the layout of the room to see how I can alter it to foster good behaviour.

Another practitioner enters her classroom on her knees once every few weeks, to see what the environment looks like to a young child. As a result of her first viewing of her setting from a child's level, she had all her display boards moved down by several feet. Other ways to assess the environment include asking a new or temporary practitioner to give you feedback about how easy she found it to work with your children, or seeing if a different group of children can tidy up successfully.

Display

 I do paintings for Angela to put on the kitchen wall. I use lots of red because it's my favourite colour. I think Angela likes it too.

Bonnie, aged four

Many practitioners find that when they begin to use brain-based learning techniques, they find themselves questioning long-held beliefs about displaying children's work. Your purpose for display will differ according to individual circumstances. However, in any setting display should:

 Create a sense of belonging

 Motivate towards further learning

 Enhance learning

 Aid recall

Invite children to be interactive

 Celebrate and affirm success

 Stimulate further thinking

 Remind of rules and behavioural codes

 Help children to make connections between concepts

For many young children, their first painting on the wall marks an important moment: they now 'belong' in this community. Their painting is there, with their name emblazoned upon it to prove that they belong. It is usually a mistake to wait until Friday to display the work done during the week. A rapid system is needed to mount work and get it on the walls while the memory is still fresh in the children's minds. Time spent in advance on preparing display boards means that display can be more immediate and meaningful for the children.

In addition to featuring the children's work, displays should inform and challenge children to think. They need to be interactive and enhance learning. They need to be three-dimensional! Young children often need to touch in order to fully understand. Tactile experience is essential to their learning. A piece of brightly coloured fabric thrown over a table or over a pile of sturdy cardboard boxes arranged at different heights can be used to make these displays.

The Thinking Child

Brain-based learning for the foundation stage

The items for these three-dimensional displays need to be exciting – but this does not mean that they necessarily have to be exotic. Most artefacts can be used in many different contexts. For example, a lavender candle given to you by an elderly aunt last Christmas could be incorporated into a display about light, or one about festivals, or colours, or shape, or materials. A mention in a newsletter to parents saying that next week you intend to make a display about insects or fish can yield some fascinating artefacts!

Captions and pictures on cards can be used to generate interest and deeper thinking. One practitioner would set challenges on caption cards, such as 'Can you find out how many legs a spider has?' The answer would be written under a flap. A parent would often work with individuals or pairs of children to read the captions and respond, and the captions would be updated regularly to increase the level of challenge. After a while, the children started to make their own caption cards. This involvement of children in the process of building displays gives them an increased sense of ownership. Including fiction and non-fiction books in displays helps to foster a sense of reading for purpose. Children soon learn to pick out relevant books and other items of interest and add them to the display. Stands that display the appropriate page of a book help children to work independently.

You also need to allow space to display affirmation posters. Ask children to help to make them and then put them up. Refer to them frequently. Likewise, posters about skills such as 'good sitting' and 'good listening', or about group rules or codes of behaviour help reinforce positive learning behaviours. Other posters can celebrate the successes of individuals and groups. Photographs can be powerful and personal reminders of success, in addition to fostering a sense of community and belonging.

Find out more about 'good sitting' and 'good listening' on page 73.

Many practitioners assign an area for children to display their own work. Here the children can be as creative as they wish. The paper, cutting and sticking materials for display can be made freely available. Depending on the age and maturity of the group, children can be taught how to use equipment, with adults then being available when they need to put their work up. The decision about how to display the work should be left to the children. They can be encouraged to write their own messages and captions for this board too. Even if George's caption reads to an adult as 'Toor er Goerg eeg rer' to George it clearly reads, 'This is George's red car'.

Display is more challenging for practitioners who work in shared settings. Many practitioners use one side of a free-standing board to display the previous week's work, and the other side for children's own work. Interactive 3D displays can be placed in front of free-standing boards or a wall, or can stand alone on covered boxes or tables. The key in these situations is good organization, such as laminating key caption cards and posters, clearly labelling storage boxes of artefacts, keeping books categorized and ordered, and using sturdy materials that withstand being repeatedly dismantled. Using plastic wallets and pockets, shoe tidies, wardrobe organizers and clothes airing racks can help to create imaginative interactive displays.

If you work in a larger setting, it is worth considering how you could use the entire environment for display. The cloakroom areas, the kitchen, the dining hall, the library and the corridors can all be used. One practitioner used ribbons hanging from the corridor ceiling to display the letters that she was teaching, or shapes, or coloured cards, or animals. She set challenges such as, 'See if you can spot any red triangles hanging from the ceiling today.'

Writing and regularly reviewing a display policy can help you to focus on how you support children's learning through display. You might wish to consider the list on pages 66 and 67, and ask yourself how your displays address each point.

Once you have done this, you can develop your policy and think of new ways to enhance learning through the displays in your setting.

Step 2: Helping children to develop good attention skills

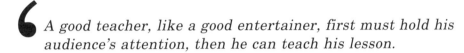

A good teacher, like a good entertainer, first must hold his audience's attention, then he can teach his lesson.

John Henrik Clarke, author, teacher and historian[35]

I like listening to stories best of all.

Aline, aged three

The development of listening skills

Good listening skills are one of the essential tools for our children as they grow and learn. Hearing is the sense that develops first in the womb, and before birth, a baby has already developed tastes in what he likes to hear. Top of the list is usually the mother's voice. Newborns will turn towards their mother at birth, and many mothers report that their babies recognize familiar music that they listened to when pregnant.

Fascinating Fact

Tests where noises are played to a foetus show that most babies respond to sound by blinking at about 24 weeks, and that the auditory pathways of the central nervous system are mature by 28 weeks.

What was not known until recently, was that hearing makes an actual physical difference to the brain:

In a child who is born deaf, the 50,000 nerve pathways that normally would carry sound messages from the ears to the brain

are silent. The sound of the human voice, so essential for brain cells to learn language, can't get through and the cells wait in vain. Finally, as the infant grows older, brain cells can wait no longer and begin to look for other signals to process, such as those from visual stimuli.

'

Ronald Kotulak [36]

Kishan's mother was worried about his hearing when he was a toddler, although hearing tests showed that there was nothing wrong. Kishan was similar to many young children: when he became absorbed in play or physical activity he tuned out the sounds around him. Many parents worry that this failure to easily process verbal communication may be a symptom of 'Attention Deficit Disorder' (ADD) or 'Attention Deficit and Hyperactivity Disorder' (ADHD). The number of diagnoses of these disorders is sharply on the rise, not just in the UK, but in most other developed nations. There are various opinions about the disorder, ranging from those who believe the symptoms to be the result of changes in parenting and society, to those who believe ADHD to be caused by mutations of specific genes.

The evidence is still too much in its infancy for us to draw firm conclusions either way. Scientists are researching to see if there are significant differences in the brains of children with an ADHD diagnosis. A study using brain imaging in 1996 by Castellanos et al.[37] showed that in ADHD children the areas of the brain that regulate attention are smaller, yet nobody knows what actually causes these differences. Castellanos hypothesized that the cause may be genetic, but others hypothesize that it is a question of cause and effect: that it is the lack of use of these areas of the brain that causes them to be underdeveloped. In other words, if children *do not practise how to pay attention*, they do not exercise that part of the brain that *enables them to pay attention*. It's rather like being unable to run because you are unfit. If you do not exercise, you will not get fit, and if you are really unfit, you will become unable to run, and so a vicious cycle develops.

The ongoing research into ADHD and consequent debate about the evidence is of particular significance to practitioners because these behaviour patterns usually surface between the ages of three and five. After all, many of the symptoms of ADHD could be argued to be simply the 'symptoms' of being four years old! Whatever the outcome of research projects, the number of children being diagnosed with this disorder is on the increase. In April 2000, BBC's *Panorama* reported that in the UK, drug prescriptions for ADHD children increased from less than 16,000 prescriptions in 1995 to nearly 140,000 in 1998, approximately a nine-fold increase.[38] A recent article in *The Observer* shocked professionals. Citing research by Dr Nora Volkow from New York, it reported that:

Even in pill form, Ritalin blocked far more of the brain transporters that affect mood change and had a greater potency in the brain than cocaine.[39]

In every setting there are children who need help to learn to pay attention and respond appropriately, because they find it difficult to respond to auditory cues. Kishan is a child who benefits from being given clear instructions and being forewarned that something is about to happen. His teacher often touches his shoulder before she speaks to him. She also prefaces each instruction with his name, giving him time to turn to look at her and prepare to listen. When Kishan is outside and involved in physical activity, she often needs to put her hands on his shoulders and stoop down to his level to speak to him. She frequently turns his head towards her when she speaks. Without this help to develop the skills of attention, Kishan would be at a disadvantage in his learning.

Processing time, when children can internalize concepts, is essential for meaningful learning, particularly for children like Kishan. It needs to be built in during group and whole class sessions in order for children to process and internalize new information. Children's attention levels tune in and out on natural cycles that are partly physiological and partly dictated by their level of interest in the activity. It is important to give time for all children to process information and avoid rushing through explanations or discussion times.

Many children have difficulty in paying sustained attention due to a hearing deficit. The National Deaf Children's Society estimates that some 80 per cent of children under eight years old experience periods of temporary deafness. Hearing difficulties account for a large proportion of children on special needs registers in schools, and many more cases remain undiagnosed. It is easy to mistake hearing loss for a behavioural difficulty or for general developmental delay. Half of deaf children remain undiagnosed by the age of 18 months and one quarter of deaf children are still not diagnosed by three years.[40] This means that a great deal of responsibility lies with the practitioner to be vigilant.

Children with hearing loss can be helped by careful management, with strategies such as making sure that you have the child's attention before speaking, positioning yourself in front of the child and getting down to his level, or ensuring that you can be seen by facing towards the light.

Teaching listening skills

Listening and sitting are skills that often need to be learned just as reading or writing. Some children enter early years education with well-developed listening skills, while others do not. To listen effectively requires that the child thinks, whereas hearing simply requires the child to be in the vicinity of the speaker! It is worth taking the time to teach these specific skills and to reinforce this learning regularly. You can begin by referring to listening effectively as 'good listening' and sitting attentively as 'good sitting':

Jamie, I can see that you are doing 'good sitting'. I like the way that you have your hands in your lap. Thank you!

Marcus is quiet and ready to do 'good listening'. He is looking at my face – well done!

The principles of 'good sitting' and 'good listening' can be taught explicitly and displayed on posters on the wall. Children need to be reminded of the rules regularly. Here are some rules for 'good sitting' and 'good listening'. To do good sitting on the carpet you must:

 Put your bottom on the carpet

 Face the front

 Cross your legs

 Put your hands in your lap

To do good sitting on a chair you must:

 Put your bottom on the chair

 Face the front

 Keep all four chair legs on the floor

 Pull the chair in to the desk

To do good listening you must:

 Keep your hands still

 Look at the speaker

 Hear what is said

 Think about it

What is an acceptable noise level?

It is difficult to define what is an acceptable noise level in an early years setting. What is appropriate on one day or in one session or with one group of children, might not be appropriate at another time. The measure of whether a noise level is appropriate has to come from observing what sort of activity is going on and how successfully the children are learning. There are different noise levels that are appropriate for different areas of the setting, and for indoor or outdoor play.

A more pertinent question therefore is probably, 'Is the noise level appropriate for the activities being undertaken, and does the language being used facilitate learning?' Do children in your care know what level of talk is appropriate for each type of activity? Do they understand that it is not appropriate to shout in a library, but that it is acceptable to shout during an action game outside? Can they listen to others in circle time and wait their turn before speaking? These are social skills that will ensure that the noise level in your setting is appropriate, no matter what activity is taking place.

It is important that children are taught about the appropriate types of voice to use in varying situations. Many children will learn this naturally, but others will need explicit teaching. A useful method for doing this is to use the 'Decibel Clock'. This is a clock face which is displayed prominently at the front of the room with different types of activities described on it with the level of noise for each type of activity: silence (0), pole-bridging (1), whispering (2), quiet talking (3) and talking (4). The practitioner turns the hand to the area of the clock face to show the noise level that she expects before the children begin the activity.

Individual cards with cartoons showing the appropriate level can be given to groups or displayed in specific areas of the room such as the book corner or home corner.

Here are three more ways to teach children how to use an appropriate voice:

Use different voices when story-telling and encourage the children to practise them, such as muttering, whispering, quiet talking, calling to somebody or shouting for help.

Use fingers to show the level of noise that you expect – a closed fist means silence, one finger means pole-bridging, two means whispering and so on.

Use a chart with pictures of different sized mouths, pointing to the size that represents the level of noise that is appropriate.

Gaining and maintaining children's attention

Inexperienced practitioners often find that one of the greatest challenges is gaining and holding children's attention. In the early years setting, this is particularly challenging. Children are encouraged to work and play independently, and materials are freely available. It is difficult for children then to learn that there are times when an adult requires them all to stop what they are doing and be quiet. Persuading ten or even 20 or 30 young children to do this at the same time is a daunting task!

The golden rule used by all successful practitioners is never to continue to speak when the children are not paying attention. To accept background noise and continue to speak is to give a clear signal that background noise is acceptable. Clarity about your expectations is vitally important. If you ask for quiet, you must settle for nothing less. For the time that you are addressing the children, it is quite reasonable to expect quiet, even from very young children, although obviously, the length of time that you expect them to maintain the quiet must be appropriate to their age and developmental stage.

It is a good idea to preface a request for quiet with a warning, to give children like Kishan processing time. Just imagine watching a gripping movie at the cinema. Suddenly there is a power cut and the screen goes blank. You don't know what is happening. Will you ever see the rest of the movie? Will you ever find out what happened at the end? The emotions that you might feel in such a situation would be felt ten-fold by a child like Kishan.

If a child like Kishan is repeatedly forced to stop what he is doing without warning, one of two things is likely to happen. He may learn to conform to such rules, even though they ignore his developmental needs. Or he may find it impossible to conform, and act out his frustration in a number of ways: by having tantrums, by continuing his games quietly while seemingly co-operating with the practitioner, or by avoiding becoming focused on an activity because he half-expects it to be halted before it has begun. Luckily Kishan's practitioner always gives ample warning that an activity is due to end.

She also provides for children to return to an absorbing activity at a later time and has a table set aside especially for children to store models or pictures that represent unfinished business to busy five year olds.

An auditory cue such as a hand bell can be used to warn children that the session is soon to come to an end. Many practitioners tell children that they have ten minutes, then five, then two, then one, before asking them to stop work. One practitioner used a familiar piece of music towards the end of the day to signal that there was not much time left. This gave children a chance to wind down and finish what they were doing.

Here are four ways to obtain children's attention:

Start by clapping your hands, gradually becoming quieter and quieter until you are tapping three fingers, then two fingers, then one finger on your palm. Teach the children to copy until you silently put your hands in your lap and are ready to speak.

Start by clicking your fingers in a rhythm, encouraging the children to copy. Move your hands in circles as you do so, growing slower and quieter until you cease and are ready to speak.

Tap your chin with a finger, then make a circular motion, tapping your ears, head, mouth, nose and so on, while the children copy until you put your hands down and start to speak.

Teach the children a variety of action rhymes for gaining attention, such as:

Give me one, give me two,
Give me five, look at you,
Ready to listen, ready to see,
Ready to learn, now look at me.

Lining up strategies

 I don't want a class full of obedient children. I want a class full of co-operative children.

Mrs S. James [41]

Moving from one activity to the next, coming in from the playground or leading into assembly, lining up can present a major challenge to the inexperienced practitioner. There is often no necessity for forming a queue for moving from one place to another. In one school, children were encouraged to stand still when the bell rang, then on the second bell simply walk into the building. There was no pushing or running, quiet conversation was allowed. If formal 'lining up' is required, it needs to be recognized that lining up is a skill that often needs to be taught and practised. Any of the suggestions below can be used to help children to move in an orderly manner from one place to another:

 Line up to a familiar piece of music

 Line up while counting in ones or twos

 Line up while singing a favourite song

 Line up according to what children are wearing

 Line up while pretending to be cats, dogs, elephants or giraffes

 Line up using a song such as the one below:

This is the way we make a line,
Make a line, make a line,
This is the way we make a line,
On a cold and frosty morning.

(To the tune of *Here We Go Round the Mulberry Bush*)

Mrs James[41] also helped her class to get 'in the mood for food' in the lunch queue, with the train song below:

Coffee, coffee, coffee, coffee, (moving arms slowly like a train)

Cheese and biscuits, cheese and biscuits, cheese and biscuits, cheese and biscuits, (gradually getting faster)

Beef and carrots, beef and carrots, beef and carrots, beef and carrots, (faster)

Fish and chips, fish and chips, fish and chips, fish and chips, (very fast)

S O U P (like a train whistle, pulling the cord to stop the train)

Now that we have considered the importance of helping children to develop good attention skills, we will move on to consider how to help them to stay on task.

Step 3: Helping children to stay on task

How much time should be 'on task'?

When a teacher complains that students are 'off task' – a favorite bit of educational jargon – the behaviorist will leap to the rescue with a program to get them back 'on' again. The more reasonable response to this complaint is to ask, 'What's the task?'

Alfie Kohn [42]

We so often hear the description of children being 'on task' or 'off task' that we can fail to think about its wider implications. The practitioner's aim should be to provide a curriculum that fully engages each individual child. Her interventions should be timely so that each child spends his time engaged in purposeful activity. Her task is to intervene in an appropriate manner when she judges that concentration is waning. She may choose to re-engage the children in the activity, or to adapt or expand the activity, or to redirect the children to do something new.

The overriding aim should be to help each individual child to develop improved concentration skills across a wide curriculum. However, sometimes a child will develop a strong interest in one type of activity and may be resistant to suggestions that he participates elsewhere. For example, when Samantha was three she attended a pre-school, which was her first experience of a setting away from the home. At first, she was reluctant to settle to any activity. When no other children were playing in the home corner, she would go in there, but if another child entered, Samantha would begin wandering around the room again.

As time went on, Samantha began to play alongside other children for brief periods. She would come to sit with an adult and watch them work with the playdough or clay. Her ability to concentrate on a task in this setting was increasing. A few weeks later, Samantha started to participate in certain activities. By the end of the first term, her concentration span on activities in the pre-school setting was similar to her concentration span at home. The amount of time that she spent "on task" during these weeks of adjustment was right for her.

So the answer to the question, 'How much time should be 'on task?' is simple – it varies enormously, according to the individual child and the task.

Structuring the less formal sessions

It is a mistake to think that enforcing formal sessions upon young children will hasten their development and accelerate their learning. In fact, what happens is quite the opposite. To provide a curriculum that is not appropriate to the age and developmental stage of the child is to inhibit his learning. That is not to say that the early years practitioner cannot ask for short periods of sustained concentration. One of her targets can be to increase the levels of concentration in individual and group work, and she can make interventions that help children to develop their concentration skills.

Carrie sometimes finds it difficult to settle at an activity for a sustained period. She often moves away before completing a task. Today Carrie is playing an imaginative game on the floor mat with the toy vehicles. She begins by lining up some of the buses at the bus station. Before she has made a line of more than four buses to be washed at the car wash, she has started to sort out the lorries into the car park. Before she has sorted more than six lorries, she has moved away to rummage in another box for some lions.

And so Carrie's game would continue, flitting from one idea to the next, if the teacher did not step in. The buses would not get washed, the lorries would never get parked and the lions would not get captured, because the policeman would have had to leave to chase the elephants! Carrie's game is elaborate and imaginative, but she needs some help to follow a theme through. Her teacher sits down to talk about the buses. 'Oh, they are lined up to go through the car wash,' she says. 'What about the lorries? Are they muddy too? Where have they been today?'

'I know,' says Carrie, able to think clearly now that she has slowed down. 'The lorries could do this....' The teacher helps her to use her imagination in a more constructive and rewarding way.

The timetable in Carrie's nursery classroom allows for plenty of opportunity for free play. The outdoor area is used throughout the day; there is no set playtime and children can choose freely whether to play inside or out. Short periods of time are set aside each day for structured group activities and music and story times. As the year progresses, children are gradually introduced to the more formal aspects of a school day. By being provided with an age-appropriate curriculum, the children develop at a natural and comfortable pace. It is a wise practitioner who realizes that development and learning go hand in hand and can be facilitated, not forced.

Introducing the more formal sessions

These are potentially confusing times for practitioners. The *Guidance on the Organisation of the National Literacy Strategy in Reception Classes* states that:

Teachers need to make arrangements to ensure that all children are introduced appropriately to the Literacy Hour and have experience of a complete literacy hour by the end of the third term in reception. [43]

Meanwhile, it states in the *Guidance on the Organisation of the Daily Mathematics Lesson in Reception Classes* that:

Towards the end of the Reception year, it is important that the lesson structure gradually becomes more like that of lessons in Years 1 to 6. This will mean longer periods of whole class teaching and children working in groups simultaneously. Over time, the elements of the daily mathematics lesson can be drawn together to form a 45 minute lesson. [44]

Considering the wide range of types of early years settings and differences in school admission policies, the question that should be foremost in the minds of practitioners is this: 'How can I meet these requirements, while taking into account the range of age and experience and maturity of the children in my setting?' Practitioners need to keep in mind that the examples given in the original framework *'illustrate what the oldest Reception children should be able to do by the end of the year.... A child who reaches the age of five in the autumn term and spends three terms in Reception.'*

As children transfer from the foundation stage to Key Stage 1, is it too much to expect all children in reception class to work on numeracy or literacy for 45 minutes or an hour each?

The answer has to be that for some children, even by the summer term, full structured sessions are too long, but for other children they are appropriate. Thankfully, the *Curriculum Guidance for the Foundation Stage* gives ample scope for creative use of the time assigned for literacy and numeracy. It is vital that the delivery of the session is appropriate to the developmental needs of young children and takes into account their short attention span. Many reception teachers, sensitive to the individual needs of the children in their care, decide to delay the introduction of the full sessions for summer-born children, boys, children with English as an additional language or those who still need a less structured approach, simply working towards giving children one experience of the full session by the end of the year. Each setting is working within different parameters and many children do not spend three terms in reception. The practitioner must work within the parameters of her setting, while being sensitive to the needs of the individual children.

For those older children who are ready for the introduction of these sessions, the simple structure described below can be used to help to fully engage young children with comparatively short attention spans.

The brain-based learning circle

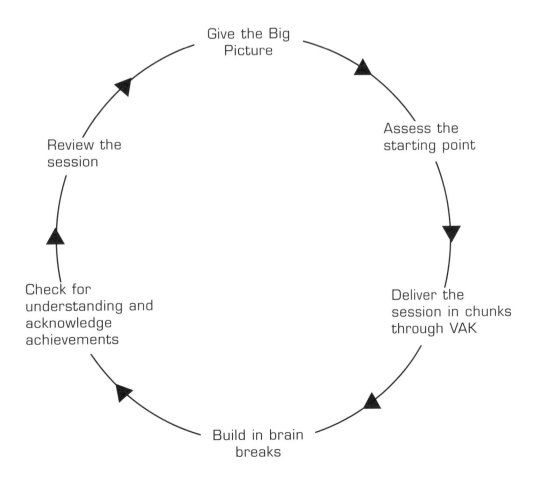

Give the Big Picture. This is an overview that is given at the start of the session. At this point it is important to ask open-ended questions and engage children's curiosity. It is also essential to allow time for processing of information. Giving visual cues helps the visual learners. Clear repetition of key phrases helps the auditory learners. Using gestures or props helps the more kinesthetic learners. Give information in short 'sound bites' and when you have given the Big Picture, check for understanding. This can be done in various ways. One method is to use the 'Traffic Light' system where the children are asked to equate their level of understanding to a traffic light. Green means 'I understand', amber means 'I'm not sure', and red means 'I don't understand yet'. For the youngest children this could be simplified and only the red and green lights used. Once you are sure that all the children understand what the session will entail, you can move on.

Assess the starting point. This ensures that the session builds on what has gone before. Getting input now from children allows the practitioner to connect their ideas to previous experiences and draw upon their current knowledge. Each child has some sort of prior understanding that he or she brings to an experience. Every starting point is different. For example, when Samantha's teacher begins a literacy session on Cinderella, Samantha and Kishan bring very different understandings to the session. Samantha went to see Cinderella at the pantomime last Christmas. The story was somewhat untraditional, and her memory is predominantly of bright lights, lots of laughter, and an exuberant dame getting dressed to go to the ball. Kishan has a copy of the book at home. He just remembers the ugly sisters trying to squeeze their ugly toes into the shoe!

Deliver the session in chunks through VAK. It is essential that practitioners break the longer sessions down into smaller parts, giving attention to the transition between activities. The crude rule of 'age plus or minus one minute' can be used for gauging children's attention span. This means that a four year old will have a focused attention span of between three and five minutes, whereas a five year old's attention span would be between four and six minutes. But of course, there is no substitute for a practitioner's judgement as to when children are wandering off task! Sessions should be planned with VAK (visual, auditory and kinesthetic learning) in mind in order to cater for the varied learning styles of individual children.

Build in brain breaks. For young children physical movement is essential for learning. Brain breaks can be planned or spontaneous. For example, in this session the reception teacher leads the children in role-play activities to break up the session. At one point, the children get down to scrub the floor and experience Cinderella's despair. At another point, they struggle to fit on an imaginary shoe that is three sizes too small. These brain break activities serve two purposes: they provide opportunities for physical reprieve, and they enrich the experience of the children.

Check for understanding and acknowledge achievements. Throughout the session you will have been observing and assessing children's understanding and progress. Now is the time to clarify and consolidate your findings, and to acknowledge what has been achieved. This may be by simply discussing what has been learned with the group or to individuals. Or it may involve one practitioner making a note of what is said as another questions the group. After the session, the team may wish to have a more formal discussion about their observations and maybe enter the information on children's records. The most significant individual and group achievements should be briefly acknowledged here, maybe by taking a moment to celebrate with a bow or a clap or a 'well done' song.

Review the session. Review should take place continually – at the end of activities, at the end of more formal sessions, at the end of the morning, at the end of the day, and at the end of the week. Each review should contribute to the ongoing To Do list in the classroom.

Step 4: Talking the language of learning

The language of the child

One of the most influential pieces of research on the language and learning of young children was that by Betty Hart and Todd Risley at the University of Kansas.[45] They found that:

'..a child from an advantaged, educated home will hear something like 700,000 affirmations by age four – parents affirming: 'You're doing something an adult finds important and interesting.' A child from a welfare family will hear about 100,000 affirmations by age four.' [46]

The researchers measured the IQ levels of the children in the study and found that the parents' education, social status, race or wealth were not as significant as the quality of language used within the home. While the definitions of 'types' of families in this study may be somewhat contentious, the results are quite clear. There are wide differences between the amount and quality of language that children experience, and the impact of this exposure to language will affect levels of attainment.

The quality of interactions that a child has, both at home and within the setting, impacts his set of beliefs about himself as a learner, which in turn impacts achievement. The nature of the child's talk will often be the deciding factor about how effectively the child learns. The practitioner needs to take care not to 'talk down' to children who might seem less articulate because they are less socially comfortable than some of their peers. She needs to take time to listen to how children interact with their parents and carers. She needs to intervene when she hears negative self-talk and work to foster positive interactions and attitudes towards learning. In short, positive self-talk leads to positive learning.

Fostering positive self-talk

Using explicit language about desirable behaviours and qualities is the key to helping children to use that language for themselves and about themselves. Language gives power to positive thinking. In a roundabout way, when explicit comments and affirmations are used about positive attributes, the behaviours often change to fit their new descriptions! Think about the power of the comments, 'Carrie, you are such a gentle girl. Jonah was so lucky to have you there to help him up when he fell off the bicycle,' or, 'You are always so kind, George. Thank you for carrying my heavy bag all this way.' Being explicit about such qualities gives children the vocabulary to describe themselves positively.

One practitioner played games where she made badges for children to wear that were printed with positive adjectives about themselves. The group would discuss the meanings of the adjectives before starting work, and she would reinforce the meanings through the day. 'Jomoke is cutting out her picture so *carefully*,' she would comment, 'that's why her badge says "careful Jomoke".' Gradually the children began to incorporate these adjectives into their own vocabulary, and would make positive comments about themselves and their friends.

For some children, intensive work has to be done to rebuild damaged self-esteem. It is the adult's responsibility to find creative and explicit ways to constantly 'talk up' achievements for these children. One teacher used circle time to create opportunities for children to say positive things about themselves. She called this the 'Blow your own trumpet' game. The children would hand around a trumpet, and after giving a good blow on it, would have the chance to tell the group something that they had achieved that day, or something they most liked about themselves, or something that they believed they would achieve soon. The teacher found that as the children became accustomed to the game, they became less self-conscious. Eventually they would 'blow their own trumpets' at other times, and would accept positive compliments about themselves without showing discomfort.

The Thinking Child

Brain-based learning for the foundation stage

Here are more ways to help children to develop positive self-talk:

 At the start of a session, talk about the qualities that would ensure success

 At review time, reflect on the reasons for children's successes

 Write stories and accounts of the positive things that happen during the day

 Make connections to children's individual personalities when reading stories

 Display photographs with captions to record positive events

Pole-bridging

One of the most effective methods of enriching and accelerating learning is called 'pole-bridging.' Pole-bridging is talking your thoughts aloud, describing what you are doing as you actually do it. Young children do this quite naturally as they play, until they become aware that talking to yourself is not always socially acceptable! But pole-bridging is a valuable skill that should be encouraged.

When Carrie pole-bridges, she needs to pay close attention to what she is doing. She needs to find the language to fit the experience by noticing details, hypothesizing, analysing and reflecting. Linking language to the experience helps her brain to lay down neural pathways. Connections are made between the language sites and other areas of the brain. When this is practised repeatedly, the connections become stronger and the neural pathways are laid for life. Imagine a jumble of telephone wires, connecting houses together all over a city. As more and more traffic travels along the most popular routes, the wiring has to be made wider and stronger. That is what is happening to the important pathways in Carrie's brain.

Today Carrie is pole-bridging as she plays in the sand pit.

Pole-bridging is helping Carrie on the way to becoming metacognitive. Metacognition is when you are not simply aware of what you are learning: you are aware of *how* you are learning. This is one of the most valuable aspects of self-knowledge for effective learning.

The language of the adult

 A teacher affects eternity; he can never tell where his influence stops.

Henry Adams, American author, 1838–1918

Keeping it positive

The language that is heard by young children is probably the greatest influencing factor upon their self-esteem and motivation. Think about the difference between, 'Amrit, walk. We don't run on the stairs!' and, 'Amrit, I was telling Mrs X how beautifully you can walk down the stairs.' There is a magic about making positive statements: children generally respond by displaying the positive behaviour that you describe, rather than the negative one that might have been their first inclination! One special needs teacher used the words, 'about to' with her group of very challenging children. 'I'm so pleased to see that David is about to sit in his chair', she said. David, who until then had very little intention of sitting in his chair, looked at her in surprise and sat down in his chair!

It is important to be vigilant about how you respond to boys as opposed to girls. Research shows that boys often behave differently to girls, even when the practitioner does not perceive this to be the case. A QCA study into boys' underachievement in English found that when given a choice:

From a young age, boys choose to spend more time on activities which do not involve adults, and this affects the nature of their relationships with teachers and helpers. In general, boys prefer active pursuits and may find it harder to acquire the more sedentary skills of reading and writing. [47]

The researchers found that one of the keys was for teachers to work hard to engage the boys in active learning:

Boys respond well to clearly set tasks with well-defined outcomes. Boys respond to strong and enthusiastic teaching.

One strategy for avoiding the gender trap is to ask a colleague to keep count of the number and type of interactions that she sees you engaged in with boys or girls. She can keep a notepad in a pocket or attached to her belt, and tick under the 'Boy' or 'Girl' column whenever she notices an interaction taking place. She can also add a 'D' for giving a direction, an 'A' for using *The Three A's*, or a 'Q' for asking or answering a question. An analysis will later show whether or not your teaching has a gender bias.

Good questioning strategies

Asking George a good question as he mixes the red paint with the blue and sloshes it over two well-glued cereal boxes and all over himself, is a skill that many practitioners have down to a fine art. However, our instinct might be to ask why on earth he was painting the box before it had a chance to dry, or even worse, to ask him to go and wash his hands quickly before he covers the rest of the clean table with his gluey painty mess!

It sometimes helps to pause for a moment and put yourself in George's shoes. George hasn't yet discovered that a thin smearing of glue will do the job better than his ample application, and besides, spreading glue is hugely satisfying. George also doesn't realize that if he covers the glue with wet paint, the boxes will most likely slip apart and will not stick at all.

George's key-worker stands back for a moment to observe what he is doing. She notices how he deliberately takes the blue brush and layers blue paint over the red, and she conjectures that possibly he has learned that when he mixes red and blue paint he has made purple.

Here is a model for good questioning strategies:

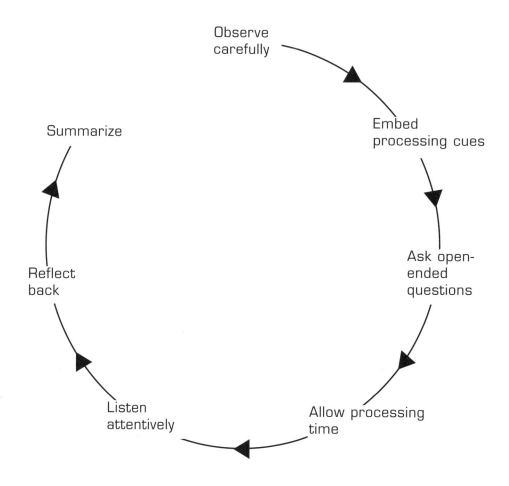

The first step to take when you are questioning a child about his learning is to *observe carefully* what he is doing or has done. Look beyond what is obvious. In this instance, the practitioner needs to look beyond the mess and notice how George is experimenting with colours. Next, as you go to ask your question, *embed processing cues* to help the child to absorb what you are saying. A processing cue gives the child time to process your question, for example, 'George, when you've put the paintbrush back I'd really like to ask you about the colours you mixed.' George has time to think about what he has discovered.

As you structure your *question*, make sure that it is *open ended*. An easy way to do this is to consider if the child is likely to give a one-word answer. If the practitioner asks George, 'Can you tell me about the colours that you were using?' George has many options open to him. The question allows him to tell her in his words what he discovered and opens the way to a more detailed discussion.

When you have asked your question, pause to *allow processing time*. This is especially important with the younger children. As a crude rule, the younger the child, the longer the processing time should be. This gives time for the child to absorb the question, formulate an answer and put it into words. Sometimes he may need to search for a word, and at this point, it is essential that he is not interrupted. The child is absorbed in his thought process, and a silence is generally not uncomfortable to him, so avoid being tempted to fill in his gaps! This is when you need to give him your full attention and *listen attentively*. George told the practitioner that the blue paint kept running off the box, and she remained silent as he added, 'I couldn't keep it on!' She realized that this had been a source of frustration to him.

Next, *reflect back* on what the child has said to you. 'That must have been frustrating, when the blue paint kept slipping off,' the practitioner could respond to George. 'Hmm, I wonder what we could do to make that paint stay on?' George's frustrations have been recognized, and together he and the practitioner can solve the problem. 'We could take some water out,' says George. 'How?' responds the practitioner. 'I don't know,' says George, and pauses, then adds, 'It can't.' 'No, it can't,' agrees the practitioner. George shrugs. He doesn't have another suggestion.

The practitioner *summarizes* the discussion, and makes a suggestion. 'But you know what, to stop the paint being so runny, we could always add more powder to the pot!' she says. 'Do you think that might work? Would you like to get the powder and we could try?'

Giving effective feedback

Feedback should help the child to refocus if he is losing concentration. It should boost his confidence if he needs reassurance. It should help him to get back on track if he has lost his sense of direction. It should lead him to further learning if he has reached a plateau. It should reinforce positive experiences and help him to avoid negative ones. It should help him to deal with possible failure by embracing challenge.

A good model for ensuring that feedback is effective is to use the mnemonic of POSITIVE.

P ersonal – make it personal by using the child's name to preface your comments. Refer back to what he has achieved before.

O bjective – give the child an impartial view about his achievements. Make sure that your response is not influenced by your expectation of what he usually achieves.

S pecific – ensure that what you say is specific to that child and that activity by avoiding making generalizations.

I nformative – give input that informs the child about what you notice he has achieved, and then help the child to think about what he might do next.

T imely – give feedback at an appropriate time. This may be during an activity or it may be afterwards, but don't leave it too late for the child to still be receptive.

I nspiring – inspire the child to want to find out and achieve more. Talk to him about how you might facilitate further learning.

V aried – use different modes and styles for giving feedback: adult to individual, adult to group, adult to class, in front of the class or a parent, or quietly in private.

E nthusiastic – show the child that you share his enthusiasm for learning!

It is tempting to make comments such as, 'Well done,' or, 'Super!' during busy periods. But this is not educative feedback; it is simply a 'holding' exercise. A better model is to make short but meaningful comments, for example, 'That's careful colouring round the edges, Sam!' or, 'You glued that really securely, Avni.' Such comments take only a second or two longer but they have real meaning. This can be followed up later with more detailed feedback. The message given to the child is that the adult has taken time to analyse his work and appreciate his efforts. His self-esteem is enhanced and he is likely to be motivated to build on his learning when he undertakes a similar activity.

This is an important purpose of giving feedback – the child should be encouraged to repeat the successful action or behaviour in similar contexts, or in more challenging situations in the future. Feedback should help him to clarify the learning that has taken place and make connections with what has gone before and what he might want to explore or attempt later. He should be encouraged by the experience to think more deeply and then be motivated to learn and achieve more.

For young children, it is important that feedback is given frequently during the experience or close to the experience. There is also value in revisiting what has been discussed during a feedback session sometime later, when an activity is about to be repeated. Plenary sessions need to be built into the day to allow adequate time for feedback from practitioner to child, child to child, child to group, or group to group. During these sessions, it is important that careful attention is paid to the balance of adult-to-child talk, and the balance of talk between the genders.

Feedback is part of a learning loop.

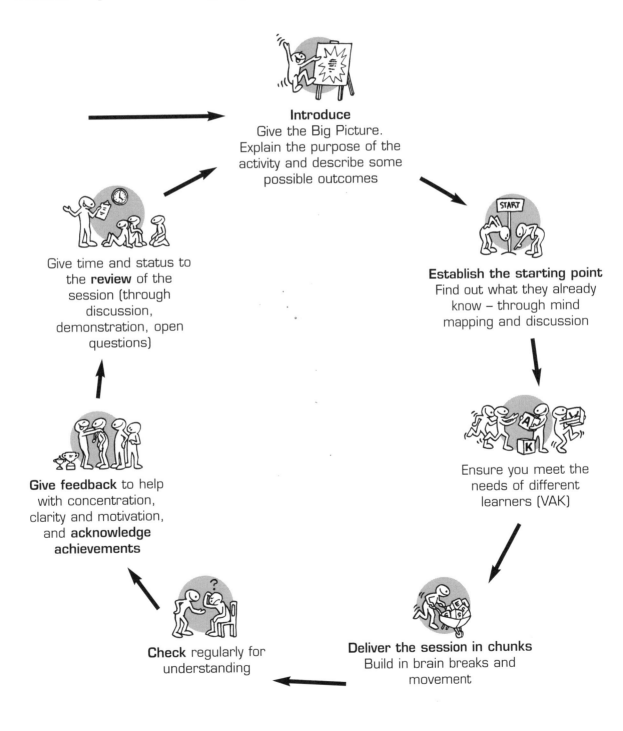

Introduce
Give the Big Picture.
Explain the purpose of the
activity and describe some
possible outcomes

Establish the starting point
Find out what they already
know – through mind
mapping and discussion

Ensure you meet the
needs of different
learners (VAK)

Deliver the session in chunks
Build in brain breaks and
movement

Check regularly for
understanding

Give feedback to help
with concentration,
clarity and motivation,
and **acknowledge
achievements**

Give time and status to
the **review** of the
session (through
discussion,
demonstration, open
questions)

Some points for reflection:

How might you want to re-organize any areas within your setting in order to implement any new techniques? Are there any areas that are wasted space? Are there any changes that you wish to make to your policy on display in order to maximize children's learning?

How good are the attention skills of the children in your setting? Do any children need help to improve their skills in 'good sitting' or 'good listening'? How might you do this?

What are the expectations within your setting for children's length of time on task? Are these appropriate demands? How might you help individual children or the group to improve their concentration span and listening skills?

If you did an audit of the language used by adults in your setting, how much of it would be positive? What about the language of the children? How might it be made more positive? How could you improve your skills in giving effective and positive feedback?

When the language used in the setting is positive, the environment is organized for maximum learning, and strategies are in place to help all children to focus and develop good listening skills, the scene is set for successful learning.

There are some special techniques that can then be used within a play-based curriculum to make the learning even more effective and exciting. That is where we head in Part Three, where you will discover some specific brain-based techniques for learning.

Developing brain-based techniques

In this section you will:

1. Learn about mind mapping, discover how to teach children to map, and learn why mapping skills come naturally to young children;

2. Consider the importance of play and think about how to ensure that your setting provides a balance of different types of play for all children;

3. Read about recent research into the connection between music and learning and learn some practical ways to use music to enhance learning for young children;

4. Discover why movement is essential for learning and learn about the specific types of movement that enhance learning in the early years;

5. Read about the necessity of monitoring the use of technology, and consider the use of a wide range of technology in the early years.

Step 1: Teaching children to mind map

What is mapping?

Mapping is a skill that comes naturally to young children and is one of the most powerful tools that can be used to enrich and accelerate learning. The power of mind mapping has commanded attention in the education world since the original work by the author Tony Buzan.[48] A mind map is rather like a spider diagram or a flow chart.

The key word – the topic – of the map is written in the middle, supported by a symbol or diagram if required. The map then develops from the centre outwards, with key words or symbols joined by lines or arrows to show the connections. The key words can be reorganized as ideas evolve, and colours and symbols can be used to represent certain categories. For example, in a map about animals the mapper might draw a green dot next to all farm animals and a red dot next to all pets. A dog might then feature in two places – as a working farm animal and as a pet, so it would require both, a green and a red dot.

> *For the first time in the three and a half million year history of human intelligence, that very intelligence has realised that it can understand, analyse and nurture itself.*
>
> Tony Buzan[48]

The map can be drawn and redrawn, or built and rebuilt. It needs to make sense to the mapper, who can talk other people through his map and explain the connections that he has made. Children find it easy to map. It is not a skill that needs to be taught as much as one that needs to be encouraged. Often mind mapping is referred to as 'memory mapping', but particularly in the early years it should be seen as a way to link ideas and concepts and engage thinking, rather than an aid to memory. For that reason, we use the term 'mind mapping' as opposed to 'memory mapping' in this book.

Young children are usually eager to describe in great detail, for example, a model that they have made. They often make complex connections, drawing together unique aspects of their lives and learning experiences. Mind mapping connects right and left hemispheres of the brain. When a young child creates a mind map, his brain is forming connections, which the adult then helps him to translate in concrete terms onto the map. Each stimulus causes electro-chemical activity and activates connections between different brain cells. If the child is asked to make a similar map on another occasion, some of the same pathways will be activated, along with some new ones. As the child's experiences build his understanding, the connective pathways will become more firmly fixed.

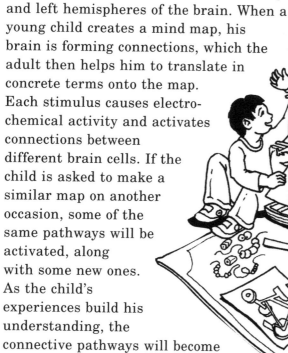

In one nursery class, the practitioner made real-life 3D mind maps with her class. On the carpet area they mapped their understanding of the topic 'Toys'. Using real toys, pictures and props, they categorized the toys and made links between concepts. Strips of card were used to link ideas. For example, an area of the mat was dedicated to wooden toys. A picture of an old-fashioned wooden tricycle was laid in that area, along with some wooden beads, bricks and toy cars. The word 'wood' was printed large in the middle of these items, along with a picture of a tree. At the end of the activity, all the labels and items were put in a box. In subsequent sessions, the mind map was laid out in slightly different ways with further items added. Children could choose to re-create the mind map themselves as an activity during the day. Later it was copied onto paper and displayed.

Mind maps need to be displayed where they are easily viewed and accessible. As new ideas emerge, they should be written directly onto the map, or on a post-it note. When children are mapping, you can be confident that they are making connections and building new concepts.

Five steps to mapping

1 Gather the children on the floor in a semi-circle. Talk about the topic for the map. It is often easier to make your first map a hands-on 3D map, so write the topic on a big label and lay it in the centre. Draw a simple picture next to the word to show its meaning.

2 Now start to build the map by asking children what they can remember about the topic. Write the key words on small pieces of card, along with a symbol or picture. You may want to have a supply of pictures already prepared to use. However, be careful not to over-direct the activity – your aim is to engage the children in building the map.

3 Ask children to fetch items that illustrate their ideas whenever practical. For example, a toy cat or dog can be placed on the map or a wooden brick next to a plastic brick.

4 Next, use strips of card or paper, or lengths of wool or string, or if you are outside, use playground chalk, to connect the ideas and link concepts. Encourage the children to get up and help to build the map, and to talk about what they are doing.

5 When the 3D map is complete, you can either dismantle it, or leave it out for children to work on through the day. You can draw it out on a large piece of card to be displayed and revisited. Alternatively, you might want to take a photograph of the map for the children to refer to. At a later stage you may wish to make the map again, in order to extend the children's thinking. The maps can form a useful part of your assessment of children's understanding.

It is also valuable to use mapping techniques to enhance your own practice, for example, for planning. Many practitioners are experienced in working this way, referring to these plans as 'brainstorms' or 'theme plans'. The value of mind mapping is that one area of the curriculum or environment does not become detached from the others. Links can be made between curriculum areas because the whole plan is on view and all practitioners can contribute. Items from the To Do lists can be incorporated, and when the map is complete the information can be considered in the light of the principles of brain-based learning, for example by asking which activities encourage a 'can-do' attitude, or how music will be used to enhance learning. Later the mind map can be used as a record of what has been achieved, linking into record-keeping systems.

Once mapping is being used comprehensively by children and adults in your setting, you can be sure that you are all working in the way that nature and evolution intended.

Step 2: **Adventures in play**

Playing with a purpose

  *Imagination is more important than knowledge. Knowledge is limited. Imagination encircles the world.*

Albert Einstein [49]

 Children do not make a distinction between 'play' and 'work' and neither should practitioners.

Curriculum Guidance for the Foundation Stage [50]

 I like playing in the sandpit with Joanne and Antonio.

Jess, aged three

'I'm not sending her to nursery school,' exclaimed Joanne's mother, 'they never do any work. All they do is play!'

Joanne's mother does not understand that for young children play is work, and work is play. Piaget wrote about how imaginative play helps the child to rationalize and make sense of his world. Through this play he meets intellectual and emotional needs, and prepares for life as an adolescent, then as an adult.

Each of our four children shows a healthy interest in different types of play. Their preferences alter according to their current interests and levels of development, but they are all fortunate in that they are provided with ample stimulation at home and in their various settings. Without the opportunity to explore their world through play, they would be likely to develop difficulties in forming healthy relationships.

Research on baby rats has shown that, when deprived of play, the result is disturbed behaviour as adults.[51] This must lead us to wonder what the effects are on children who are denied play opportunities in their formative years. If Daniel Goleman argues convincingly that EQ is a more influential factor determining a child's future than his IQ, then play has to be recognized as the cornerstone of early years education, because it is the one single activity that provides simultaneously for intellectual and emotional development.

In his book *Building Healthy Minds,* Stanley Greenspan describes how, in order to reach a level of 'moral consciousness', a child has to understand that actions will always have consequences.[52] For example, when George is cross because another child took his bucket and spade in the sand tray,

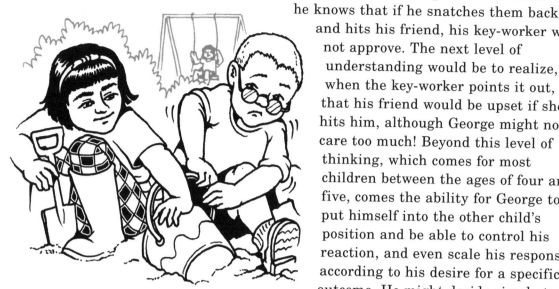

he knows that if he snatches them back and hits his friend, his key-worker will not approve. The next level of understanding would be to realize, when the key-worker points it out, that his friend would be upset if she hits him, although George might not care too much! Beyond this level of thinking, which comes for most children between the ages of four and five, comes the ability for George to put himself into the other child's position and be able to control his reaction, and even scale his response according to his desire for a specific outcome. He might decide simply to take back the bucket and spade, which will annoy his friend but not cause a fight, or he might decide to take them back with a little push, just to convey the message that he's upset. At this level, George is making a conscious decision about his response. He is developing emotional intelligence, but needs guidance to ensure that he learns to make responses that are appropriate.

Our four children went through stages that are accepted as the norm for the development of play. As a tiny baby, Samantha's play began at the functional level, as she played with her hands or repeatedly banged two blocks together. Later her play began to have more purpose as it went through the constructive stage, for example when she pushed all the shapes from her shape sorter into a tissue box. Soon her play began to take on an imaginative element as she began to engage in dramatic play. Finally, by the time she started school she could play games with basic structure and rules, although the ability to take part in organized games is one that will take some fine-tuning in the years ahead.

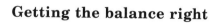

The five aspects of emotional intelligence are **self-awareness**, **management of emotions**, **self-motivation**, **handling relationships** and **empathy**.

Getting the balance right

There should be opportunities for children to engage in activities planned by adults and also those that they plan or initiate themselves.

Curriculum Guidance for the Foundation Stage [53]

Achieving the right level of adult involvement in play

Experienced practitioners judge when to become involved in play and when to let children take the initiative. It can be tempting to over-organize or dominate play. A balance has to be achieved where structure and enrichment do not become control, and spontaneous play is allowed to develop. The practitioner's role is to observe, interact, and provide for the development and enrichment of play activities. Sometimes she will need to join in the game; at other times she will simply observe and make a mental note of how she might be able to extend the learning. Occasionally she will need to intervene to help children to manage their emotions or actions within the game. Through this sort of play, children develop physically, cognitively, emotionally and socially. There are many reasons for getting involved in children's play, for example, to help children to play collaboratively, to model new language or vocabulary, or to offer ideas about how to extend the play.

It is disturbing to read reports of how some schools are cutting back on the amount of play to make more time for 'teaching'. This is a serious mistake. It presupposes that learning for young children can be better achieved if it is 'taught' rather than facilitated. It completely overrides the basic truth that young children *learn best through play*.

The intense pressures of testing, target setting, and the Literacy and Numeracy Strategies can lead to demands being made to cut back on play. Time needs to be used to maximum effect, but 'wasting time' must not be confused with *spending time* on worthwhile non-academic activity! Children need substantial periods of uninterrupted time to become engrossed in their own play. This is essential if play is to develop and grow into real long lasting learning. Researcher Jacqui Cousins from the Oxford Brookes University observed four year olds interacting with their teachers. She found that:

For most children, being stopped in the middle of the learning process was worse when little or no warning was given that a session was coming to a close. When such interruption occurred, I observed how seldom children were able to pick up the threads of their thinking or their action. [54]

Intervening in play at the right moment is vital. Making the judgement of what is the right moment is a skill that can take a lifetime to perfect – and sometimes even the most skilled practitioners get it wrong! Being aware of the purpose for getting involved means that the practitioner can make a better judgement about when it is a good idea to join in the children's learning and enrich the experience, and when it is better to allow them to create their own adventures and follow them through to their natural conclusion.

It is helpful if practitioners educate parents, carers and colleagues about play, for example by encouraging all adults to join in play activities and providing examples and documentation about the importance of play. One of the best ways to do this is to lead workshops where adults have to explore new concepts – through first-hand play experience!

Balancing indoor and outdoor environments

 A lengthy childhood keeps thinking flexible, and helps intelligence to grow.

Tina Bruce [55]

The QCA guidance emphasizes the importance of providing a learning environment which includes both indoors and outdoors. Ideally, the outdoor area should be an extension of the classroom. There should be no fixed 'playtime' and the concept of 'play' versus 'work' should not exist. In the most effective settings the outdoor area is used by groups of children, weather permitting, continuously throughout the day. Children come and go from indoors to outdoors, and themes from one area naturally extend across to others. For example, in one nursery class a group of children gardened outdoors, digging a new vegetable bed. Inside, another group of children were busy making a scarecrow to keep the birds from eating the seeds.

This type of imaginative use of the outdoor space should extend to stimulate every type of play. Some children choose to play outside, while others are more reluctant. It is important to help children to achieve a balance of different types of play, while recognizing that individual children will go through stages of preferring one type of play to another. If practitioners plan for indoors and outdoors together, it becomes easier to encourage children to take part in activities in both areas.

Tables can be set up for art activities outside, the home corner can be taken out of doors, and small world play toys can be set out on blankets in the garden. Themes can be developed for both indoors and outdoors. For example, the train set can be set out on a mat outside, while the big brick area can be set out to encourage children to build trains. If practitioners resist the temptation to think of either 'inside' or 'outside' activities, children are more likely to move from their comfort zones and take part in a wider variety of activities.

Almost all children like to spend time gardening. Digging, planting, trimming and watering plants are activities that have enormous learning potential. You don't even need a natural earthy area in order to create a garden: imaginative use of grow-bags and a variety of containers can give endless possibilities for gardening even in the most barren concrete jungle.

The key to providing a stimulating outdoor environment for young children is not necessarily to have a great deal of money to spend. It is more important to have a great deal of imagination! If you have a difficult outdoor area to organize, you will need to use even more imagination. Look for ways to link the play from indoors to outdoors, such as by using the wheeled toys as pizza delivery bikes, or by having a car wash or a parcel delivery service. Brainstorm ideas with other practitioners and visit other settings to gain ideas about how others set up their outdoor areas. If you do not have an area for children to play outside, try to make use of the school or village hall, the local park or a games field where children can run and play with their whole bodies and in freedom. Children can help beforehand to load up a wheeled trolley with a selection of play items.

Inexpensive items can be collected for use to stimulate outdoor play, such as lengths of plastic guttering and tubing for water play, large chalks to make roads and other maps for small world play, and big cardboard boxes for building buses, trains, or whatever comes into the children's minds!

It is a good idea to look also at your indoor area to check that movement and access are easy and activities are grouped in helpful ways. Taking time to observe children's play can help you to make decisions about altering the layout. The routines and systems that you use will also affect children's play. If you keep checklists to ensure that all children take part in certain activities, take care not to over-use them or make their use too explicit. If children sense that you have an agenda, for example, that everybody will take part in a finger-painting activity at some stage during the morning, their play will alter to accommodate your agenda. If you do need to organize children in this way, be sensitive to the play that is going on and keep interruptions to a minimum.

You can encourage children to extend their independent play indoors by making more than one carpet area for floor play, labelling and organizing equipment so that children can find things and put them away, and giving children plenty of notice before 'packing up time'.

> I like riding on the big red bike. If Miss Connor says I have to wait my turn, I go on the blue one instead. It's almost as good but the wheels don't turn as fast.
>
> Jake, aged four

Step 3: **Maximizing learning through music**

> My favourite song is 'Walking on Sunshine'. It makes my shoulders wiggle around!
>
> Joe, aged five

> *Music speaks in a language that children instinctively understand. It draws children (as well as adults) into its orbit, inviting them to match its pitches, incorporate its lyrics, move to its beat, and explore its emotional and harmonic dimensions in all their beauty and depth. Meanwhile, its physical vibrations, organized patterns, engaging rhythms, and subtle variations interact with the mind and body in manifold ways, naturally altering the brain in a manner that one-dimensional rote learning cannot.*
>
> Don Campbell [56]

Since the release in 1997 of Don Campbell's book *The Mozart Effect*, companies have sprung up to supply educators and parents with music and materials that are claimed to increase a child's IQ. The 'Mozart Effect' was first discovered by Drs Rauscher and Shaw from California. They discovered that students who listened to ten minutes of Mozart scored between eight and nine points higher on a spatial IQ test than those who did not listen to any music. They concluded that listening to Mozart helps to organize the firing patterns of neurons in the brain, especially those used for spatial-temporal reasoning.

Scientists can now use brain-imaging technology to study the way that different parts of the brain show increased electrical activity when the individual listens to music. Elaborate neural networks are formed in the cortex to process music. New activity is seen in the brain when the individual engages in musical tasks such as learning to play an instrument, responding to music with dancing or movement, or learning to compose music. The right and left hemispheres of the brain have to communicate to make sense of the musical experience. It has been found that the corpus callosum, which is the route for communication between the hemispheres, is often thicker in the brains of people who experienced musical training as a child. Other researchers have found a link between children's ability in musical sound discrimination and their reading ability.[57]

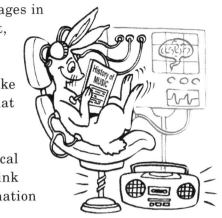

Rauscher and Shaw found in a later study that pre-school children who had piano lessons developed superior spatial-temporal skills than those who had computer training.[58] These skills are important for mathematical development, for example for understanding proportion and geometry. All this makes powerful ammunition for those who argue for providing a rich and varied musical diet for children in the early years. Don Campbell believes that the evidence indicates that:

Learning about music can be just as important to a child's intellectual and emotional development as learning to the accompaniment of music. [59]

There are many opportunities to utilize music for many different purposes, beyond the usual timetabled or organized music sessions. Music can be played to create the right atmosphere for various times of the day. For example, you might want the children to arrive in the morning in a calm, reflective mood. Or you might want to energize them after lunch, or help them to relax at the end of a hot summer afternoon.

Brain-based learning for the foundation stage

Children thrive on familiarity, so some pieces can be used repetitively for specific purposes. For example, music can be used to indicate that it is time to begin an activity. Some practitioners use the same calm piece of music each day for snack time, finding that when children hear the music they go to wash their hands and sit down without needing verbal direction. Similarly, a familiar piece can be used to signal that an activity is coming to an end. A piece of music can also be used to demarcate the time that is needed to complete a task, while injecting a sense of fun to the activity, for example at tidy-up time or when putting shoes and socks back on after PE.

Music can act as a 'vehicle' for learning basic concepts. Parents have known this instinctively for many generations. Just think about how many of us still sing the alphabet to ourselves when flicking through a dictionary! Number songs and rhymes are an essential part of the early years experience and should be included in planning to ensure a wide breadth and variety of material. Some reception teachers start numeracy sessions with a 'maths to music' session where they sing number songs, rhymes and maths songs to well-known tunes or use published tapes and CDs. It is worth considering where there might be additional times to include these songs during the day, for example, when lining up for lunch, handing out snacks or walking to the park. The use of these extra slots of time can double or even triple the children's exposure to learning through music.

Learning nursery rhymes and songs has also been shown to have an impact on later literacy development. A 1998 review of the research that underpins the National Literacy Strategy drew attention to the importance of providing this rich musical and linguistic experience for children in the early years:

Researchers have associated phonological development with early success in learning to read for some years. One of the most influential publications in this area was that by Bradley and Bryant (1983) which reported a longitudinal study of 368 children and the finding that children's sensitivity to rhyme was a particularly important predictor of subsequent success in reading. [60]

Variations of popular songs and nursery rhymes can be used with young children to help to give structure to routines, and even to help to maintain a cheerful atmosphere while doing chores! For example, one nursery nurse used this adaptation of the song *There was a Princess Long Ago* to make tidy-up time go with a swing:

We are the helpers in this room, in this room, in this room,
We are the helpers in this room,
In this room.

Then,
We put the aprons on their hooks
We put the bricks back in the box
We put the tops back on the pens — and so on!

Finally, music can be used to increase the sense of joy when celebrating the children's achievements. One practitioner used Louis Armstrong's *What a Wonderful World* as a background for a regular Friday afternoon celebration. The children knew that when they heard the song begin, they should get ready to congratulate one another on a great week's work.

As the children in your care engage in exciting learning adventures, their experience can be made all the more exciting and enriching through the imaginative use of music. When movement is added to the experience, the learning can be even more effective. Using movement to enhance and accelerate children's learning is what we move on to consider in the next chapter.

Fascinating Fact

Even plants prefer classical music! A researcher from Denver conducted an experiment with five greenhouses of plants to see if music affected their growth. After several months, the plants that had listened to Bach and Indian music were thriving, and the vines even grew towards the speakers. The country-western listening plants were almost identical to those in the greenhouse that had no music. Sadly, the plants in the rock'n'roll greenhouse did not do well; there were fewer flowers and their growth was poor. [61]

Step 4: Teaching and learning through movement

The more closely we consider the elaborate interplay of brain and body, the more clearly one compelling theme emerges: movement is essential to learning.

Carla Hannaford [62]

The young child needs to interact with his world in a physical way in order to make sense of it. The early years curriculum should provide the opportunities for freedom of exploration and movement. The amount that a young child will move during a day can be staggering. An Olympic athlete once described an experiment where he was asked to 'shadow' a two year old for a day. By the end of the day he was more exhausted than after a full day's training at the athletic track! He could not believe how many miles a toddler could cover – at top speed – in a day!

Three, four and five year olds have developed a longer concentration span than a toddler. By this age, most children are capable of learning when and where it is appropriate to move or to sit still. As children mature, the demands upon them to stay focused can gradually increase. However, movement still needs to be built into sessions where children are required to sit and focus. There are several reasons for this.

Each of us learns through a variety of strategies. These can be crudely categorized into three types: visual, auditory and kinesthetic, or, 'seeing, hearing and doing'. It is this 'doing' part that involves movement. You can probably picture a child with a strong preference for kinesthetic learning. He or she is the one who will typically fidget during quiet times, and want to be the first to get hold of the instruments in music or the props in circle time. He or she will generally be found participating in exploratory, practical activities. Rarely will the kinesthetic child choose to sit and listen to an adult's explanation or watch a new skill demonstrated, preferring to have a 'hands-on' experience.

There are physiological reasons why movement should be built into each session through regular brain break activities. Aerobic movement increases the oxygen supply to the brain, which uses about one fifth of the body's oxygen supply. Movement also reduces stress. Stress increases the amount of cortisol in the system. Cortisol is not useful if we want a child to be in a calm and positive mood for learning. In addition, exercise seems to increase the body's production of *neurotrophins*, which stimulate nerve cell growth and increase neural connections.

Movement can enhance activities such as helping children to learn to write their names, form letters correctly or spell simple words. Children enjoy writing their names in the air with their hands or with a magic wand, or even a silly prop like a carrot! They should be encouraged to write slowly with left hand, right hand, and then both hands, and with their eyes open and then with their eyes closed. As a fun variation, they can then write with their feet on the floor in front of them. Adding movements to songs and rhymes aids language development and the understanding and recall of new vocabulary.

There is now evidence that specific types of controlled, organized series of cross-lateral movements can help with learning by connecting both hemispheres of the brain and strengthening neural pathways. This type of movement, known as 'Brain Gym'®, is described in the book *Smart Moves:*

Cross lateral movements, like a baby's crawling, activate both hemispheres in a balanced way... Because both hemispheres and all four lobes are activated, cognitive function is heightened and ease of learning increases. [63]

Brain Gym® activities focus on specific aspects of sensory activation and are designed to activate full mind and body functions. Practitioners who use Brain Gym® talk of significant improvements in children's concentration levels, receptiveness to learning and specific motor skills. Examples of Brain Gym® exercises for young children are cross crawling, the energy yawn or arm activation. At cross crawling, for example, children stand and alternately raise their left knee to touch their right elbow, and then their right knee to touch their left elbow. This is not as easy as it sounds! This can be done at different speeds, and little 'skips' can be added between each set. For children who find this difficult, coloured stickers on their opposite knees and hands can help. Music can be added to energize and give a real sense of fun.

Brain Gym® exercises can be timetabled for specific short brain 'workouts' during the day, or they can be used simply as fun time-fillers such as when waiting for snacks to be ready. It can be useful to create a space in your planning format to make a note of the exercises that you plan to use each week. You might wish to adapt the exercises. Popular children's songs can be adapted for brain exercises, for example, *Heads, Shoulders, Knees and Toes, Pat-a-cake, Tommy thumb* or *I'm a Little Teapot.* Rhymes for gaining children's attention can also incorporate careful deliberate movements, such as:

Point to the ceiling (right hand)

Point to the floor (right hand)

Point to the window (left hand)

Point to the door (left hand)

Point to you (both hands)

Point to me (both hands)

And sit and listen

Quietly (hands crossed on chest)

Ironically, the importance of movement for effective learning is sometimes overlooked because it is so simple. It is easier sometimes to turn to more 'modern' techniques and equipment. That is where we head next in our learning journey: to consider the use of modern technology with young children.

Step 5: **The place for technology**

 The best thing about the computer is when I get funny e-mails from Grandad with pictures on them.

Evan, aged 3

When we hear the word 'technology' in the context of education we tend to immediately think of high-tech equipment. The thinking in many educational circles is that young children should be provided with computer access, and certainly this is the current political agenda. Yet, there are many other applications of technology that are appropriate for the early years.

Our purpose should be to help children to develop knowledge and understanding about the world, which includes a wide variety of types of technology, some of which we tend to overlook because they have become so familiar to us. The world for children today is very different to the world that we grew up in, and it is likely to change even more during their lifetimes. It is our responsibility to help children to see the purposeful uses of this technology and to become competent in its use, without overlooking the essential skills and knowledge that enable them to operate independently of technology when appropriate. Put simply, if you have no concept of addition or multiplication, a calculator is useless to you. Balance, as always, is the key.

There are many ways to introduce children to ICT within the context of daily life without the use of a computer, such as teaching them to help you to set clocks and alarms for timed activities, allowing them to use the telephone under supervision, or creating a balance in cookery between making things by hand and using modern appliances.

It seems inevitable that there will come a time when almost every pre-school child is provided with access to a computer. This is certainly the aim of the government:

 If we really go ahead with this new technology, the kids will learn better and faster and will get better jobs when they leave school.

Prime Minister Tony Blair [64]

Used wisely and with discrimination, there is no doubt that computer technology can enhance learning. For example, as a tool for language and early literacy development, the word processor can be useful, while early mark making can be fostered through good paint programmes. But an emphasis needs to be placed on achieving balance, with some experts urging caution in this campaign to use increasing amounts of technology with very young children:

> *While the 'learning' gained there (e.g., knowing letters, geometric shapes, reciting the names and characteristics of all the dinosaurs) looks impressive to adults, it may be only superficial mastery. Children playing with unit blocks may not know the name of a 'rectangle,' but they have a gut-level understanding of its properties and how it works.*

Jane Healy [65]

The quality of software targeted at young children varies considerably. It is essential that practitioners look beyond the special effects or the 'cuteness' of software. Be cautious about programs that give children immediate gratification for impulsive answering. Teddies that dance when a child gets the right answer may seem cute, but if he simply hits keys randomly in order to get the 'right' answer and trigger the special effect, his learning is negligible and, moreover, he is being rewarded for impulsive behaviour. Good software requires the child to take time to think before answering. It is worth adults using each piece of software themselves in order to really analyse the learning that will take place when a child sits in front of the computer screen.

Practitioners need to consider issues such as equality of access and gender bias. It has been shown that boys come to dominate computers in the classroom from the earliest age. Research by Bergin et al.[66] in 1993 found that when grouping young children at the computer, boys invariably dominate the activity, even though at this age, girls are equally as interested in computer activities as boys. Then, as girls get older, their interest declines, suggesting that the school experience perpetuates gender bias.[67]

It is wise to have a clear policy that ensures that the use of computers in your setting enhances both learning and learning attitudes for all children. Consider questions such as, 'How do we select software?', 'Has each practitioner used and evaluated each piece of software in order to be sure of its educational value?' and, 'How do we ensure that there is equal computer access for all children?'

Children's exposure to technology will naturally vary enormously, from those children who are frequent computer users, to those who have little experience with any forms of technology, and all shades in between. The responsibility of practitioners is to ensure that they offer a healthy technological 'diet'. The key has to be to find a balance, so that technology takes a rightful place in helping children to develop knowledge and understanding of the ever-changing world in which they live.

Some points for reflection:

How could you use mind mapping in your everyday life? Have you noticed any ways that children naturally map ideas and make connections? How could you go about encouraging the children in your setting to map their ideas and findings?

Is there a balance in the types of play in your setting? Do the children use the outdoors as freely as the indoors? How could you rectify any imbalance? How do you ensure that there is a balance between adult and child initiated play?

How do you already use music in your setting? Are there ways that you could expand your use of music to enhance learning? What resources might you need? How could you introduce new ways of using music for specific purposes?

Do the children in your setting get adequate opportunity for movement? Are there times when they are expected to sit for sustained periods? Do some children find this difficult? If so, how might you help them?

How extensively do you use technology in your setting? How do you evaluate the technology diet that is on offer to the children? How might you want to review your policy? How could you increase the children's access to more varied types of technology?

Part Three

Once the specific brain-based techniques such as mind mapping and using technology, music and movement for learning are incorporated into a stimulating and balanced play-based curriculum, the potential for children's learning is greatly enhanced.

Part Four

The teaching and learning can now become increasingly creative, and it can be moulded to suit the different types of intelligence and learning styles of each unique child. This is what we will consider next: how to teach creatively for the individual children in each setting.

Teaching for intelligence

In this section you will:

1. Find out about the research into the quality of learning through different teaching styles and be given many suggestions of how to be creative in your work;

2. Consider the importance of encouraging children to co-operate in groups and consider some different ways to organize group work;

3. Read about learning through VAK — visual, auditory and kinesthetic — or 'seeing, hearing and doing', and discover ways to help each individual type of learner;

4. Learn about the 'multiple intelligences' and discover how to recognize these forms of intelligence and cater for them in your setting.

Step 1: Creative teaching for better learning

The American researcher David Weikart conducted an experiment in the 1960s involving two groups of children from poor neighbourhoods.[68] Both groups of children were educated through pre-school for exactly the same number of hours per week from the age of three to five. The difference was that one group was taught using direct instruction and rote-learning, whereas the other group was taught through active learning.

 It is the supreme art of the teacher to awaken joy in creative expression and knowledge.

Albert Einstein [69]

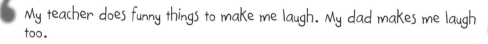 My teacher does funny things to make me laugh. My dad makes me laugh too.

Eleni, aged three

At the age of ten, the IQ levels of both groups had climbed significantly, but there was no real difference in IQ levels between the two groups. Yet by the age of 23, significant differences had begun to emerge. Of the children who had been in the rote-learning group, almost 50 per cent had needed treatment for emotional problems, 39 per cent had been arrested for a felony offence, and only 27 per cent planned to graduate from college. Of the children in the other group, only 6 per cent had suffered emotional problems, 10 per cent had been arrested for a felony, but 70 per cent planned to graduate from college.

The significance of this experiment is that even if academic test scores can be shown to be equal after widely differing types of early years education, the importance of active learning stretches far beyond academic attainment into the realms of emotional and moral well-being. We now know that the actual process of learning is as important as the learning outcome. We understand the importance of play and of providing a stimulating and exciting environment where children engage in a wide variety of activities and experiences. One of the most exciting things about working in the early years is the fact that practitioners often have the greatest of imaginations and come up with endless ideas about how to make learning exciting and fun.

One nursery teacher developed what she called the 'fantasy classroom'. She would take a theme, such as a fairy tale, and develop a fantasy with the children within the classroom – quite literally pretending that the children and staff were taking part in the fairy tale. For example, on one occasion, she built a bears' cave from

blankets hung from the ceiling for the children to discover when they arrived the next morning. Torches and tiny flashlights lay by the door to the cave, and the children gradually ventured inside to discover three fluffy bears with wet noses sitting within the cave! The next day, when the children arrived at school, they found a track of bear footprints leading from the cave to the outdoor area, and there, under a canvas cloth, were the three bears, sitting ready for a picnic. The children's play continued throughout the week as they expanded and enriched this fantasy, building furniture for the bears, making food for them, and even learning to talk 'Bear Language'.

By providing unusual activities and doing the unexpected, children's thinking can be challenged, causing them to need to draw on past experiences to make sense of the new. This is the most effective way to learn: to have a concept that is already held challenged by something new. When this happens, the child has to reconsider his current understanding of the concept and check it against new criteria. This may confirm what he already knew, or lead him to reject what he previously thought, or it might create a new level of understanding.

In order to make sure that the children in your setting are challenged by new and unexpected experiences, it can be helpful to simply move equipment and materials from one place to another, imagining how it might be used in a different context. When you are planning, take time to think about what could be done to make the activity a little more unusual. Consider how you could make an activity multi-sensory. What about adding scent to the playdough? Why not use unusual colours for the water tray: how would the children respond if the water were black or dark brown? What music could accompany an activity: how about composing a rap to sing about the *Three Little Pigs*? How could the paint be made more textured: how would the children react if you added sugar, or rice and glue to the paint pots? Get creative by putting the boats in the sand tray, filling the water tray with ice cubes or leaving a trail of strange footprints across the floor or on the path.

Children themselves are masters of original thinking. A pre-school leader told of a project that was started when Mimi, aged four, suddenly said, 'What do you think Jake-the-Peg did when he needed a new pair of wellies? How did he get enough wellies to go around all his feet?' Mimi and her friend experimented with a doll, who they called 'Jake-the-Peg', and several pairs of boots. As children engage in these unusual activities, encourage them to use language to describe their thinking. If they pole-bridge as they play, the experience will become more concrete and the neural pathways that are created will become stronger. Link each experience to other concepts that have been learned, and then plan what could be investigated later. Making a mind map in the plenary session, then revisiting it at a later times is one of the most effective ways to do this. Allow children to suggest further ideas for their To Do list, and so build upon their ability to think creatively and take charge of their own learning.

The brain-based learning environment is one that is never static. It is exciting and it challenges the thinking of adults and children alike. Original thinking is encouraged and celebrated. Children and adults learn together.

Step 2: **Fostering the beginnings of group work**

 A mind that is stretched by a new experience can never go back to its old dimensions.

Oliver Wendell Holmes [70]

The importance of group work now commands a lot of attention in education circles. If children can learn to co-operate with peers in the early years, the skills can be set for lifelong learning. Studies have shown that the quality of language and interaction improves dramatically when practitioners use good group work strategies. A study by Judith Watson[71] from the University of Edinburgh in 1999 found that the increase in classroom talk could be as much as from 5 per cent to 40 per cent when teachers were skilled in fostering co-operative learning.

During the foundation stage, there is naturally a mixture of time spent in different types of groups. Much of the time the groups are self-selected, or simply occur through circumstance: if three children choose at any one time to play in the sand, then that group might engage in co-operative play. However, five minutes later, another child may join them and two of the original group may leave. The balance of time spent in different formations of groups will largely depend on the organizational aims of the practitioner. Sometimes she might gather together a specific group of children to take part in an activity, but at other times, the group that evolves will be determined by the children themselves.

When we add into this scenario the fact that children will be passing through various developmental stages of play, we can see that the early years setting has numerous possibilities for group work. As children pass through the various stages of play, they will first only engage in solitary play. Then they will begin to play alongside other children in parallel play, and then engage in associative play before finally being able to play co-operatively with their peers. This will not necessarily be a linear progression. All children in the early years will be at some stage on the continuum between playing alone and working confidently in a group, and it is the job of the practitioner to organize activities that help children to develop the strong social skills that group work demands.

In George's pre-school, social skills are fostered through the children being given opportunities to become involved in the organization and running of the setting. In addition to the usual expectations of children to help to tidy the room at the end of the session, the staff find ways that the children can help with additional tasks. For example, when the staff decided to wash all the outdoor play equipment, they made it into an activity in which the children participated. George and his friends spent a very enjoyable and rewarding morning outside working with sponges, scrubbing brushes and water.

When a child is allowed to work on these sorts of real life tasks he often has no choice but to work in a group. With a practical task to do, the child has a greater incentive to co-operate with others. It is useful to comment on the skills needed to achieve a successful outcome, such as, 'Carrie, if you help Sam by holding the dustpan as he sweeps, he will be able to get all the woodchips swept up much more easily.' By being given explicit instructions on how to succeed, children can be helped to then transfer what is learned in one  situation to another, such as, 'Good thinking, Carrie! That really helps Jimmy if you hold the bucket as he turns on the tap.' Other examples of everyday tasks that children can be involved with include washing the home corner equipment, cutting flowers and arranging them in vases, sharpening pencils or preparing snacks.

Children benefit from working in a variety of group arrangements. It is important to ensure that each child has experience of different types of grouping. Each type of grouping creates different types of language and interactions. It is important to build in lots of opportunities for children to work in pairs with a friend. This helps to build a solid grounding for learning to work in a larger group. Sometimes it might be necessary to group children of a similar stage of development together in order to teach a specific skill or concept. At other times, encouraging pairings between a child who has a good grasp of something and another child who needs practice in that area can benefit both children: the 'leading' child reinforces what he already knows and can do, while the 'following' child learns naturally from somebody his own age. Sometimes, children benefit from working with a self-selected group of friends, while at different times, it can be useful to randomly pick groups, for example by the colour or type of clothes that the children are wearing, or by hair or eye colour, or by giving out coloured stickers to children on the mat.

It will accelerate children's social development if you are explicit about the skills that are necessary for success in groupwork. A useful model for teaching the more mature children to work systematically and reflectively is to teach them to use the 'Plan, Do and Review' model. Practitioners who use High Scope methods will know this system well. This requires children to take time to think and then verbalize their actions as they work. By working with the group to make a plan, the practitioner is helping them to learn to manage the moment of impulse – to resist the temptation to grab the materials and get started! The review session after the activity gives an opportunity for the group to reflect on the way that the group worked together.

Experience of group work will enable each child to develop the skills necessary to work as a part of a team, which is a skill for success in all areas of life. Being able to work with two friends to produce a dinosaur out of the big blocks at the age of three or four, is laying the foundations for being able to work with a team of technicians to make a major medical discovery 30 or 40 years later. The early years really are the start of a major adventure in learning!

Step 3: Teaching through VAK

Visual, auditory and kinesthetic learning

Learning is experience. Everything else is just information.

Albert Einstein[72]

To have a good brain you need to be healthy and clever.

Gaby, aged five

A simple way to explain differing learning styles is to break them down into three categories: visual, auditory and kinesthetic – in other words, seeing, hearing and doing. Each individual learner has a preferred style, but it would be simplistic to suggest that each person is a visual, auditory or a kinesthetic learner. Instead, we all have a preference for learning using one of these areas, but utilize all three methods to some degree.

Kishan is clearly a strongly kinesthetic learner. He likes to engage in physical activity and is good at manipulating materials through three dimensions. By contrast, Samantha has strengths

in auditory learning. Samantha listens well, and also finds it relatively easy to follow what her teacher is writing or drawing on the whiteboard as she gives an explanation to the group.

Each child has different skills, attitudes and aptitudes. The practitioner's role is to ensure that a balance is sought where there is an equal demand upon children's visual, auditory and kinesthetic engagement. The 'workshop' type of arrangement where there are clear guidelines for the different activities in each area can help to create this balance. The timetable also needs to be monitored to ensure that there is a VAK balance. For example, story-telling sessions might suit auditory learners if tapes are used. However, if visual aids and props are added, the activity is more accessible to visual learners. If a balance of all three styles is offered over a period of time, then each child will be catered for and will have the opportunity to practise using each style of learning. Some practitioners adapt their planning formats by adding tick boxes for VAK to ensure that they provide a balance.

Your personal learning preference will affect your teaching. Many practitioners find that it is helpful to analyse their personal learning style and that of their colleagues. You also need to analyse the strengths and weaknesses of the children, and encourage them to develop all-round learning skills. The more tools a child has under her belt and the more ways that she can approach learning, the more effective her learning will be.

Visual learning

At birth, sight is one of the least developed of all the senses. It has not been practised in the womb! Everything that is not between eight and fourteen inches from a newborn's face appears as just a blur. It is not a coincidence that Carrie's mother instinctively lent to gaze at Carrie's face at a range of eight to ten inches as she nursed her. Within a few hours of birth Carrie could recognize her mother's face. Research has shown that early visual experience actually affects the wiring of the brain:

The more a baby sees, and the better that input is suited to her visual ability at that particular stage, the better she is likely to be at the many later tasks that depend on vision. Who knows? It may even make the difference in whether she ends up as an artist, or a naturalist, or an expert tennis player.

Lise Eliot [73]

Carrie does, in fact, have a strong visual memory. She amazed her mother before the age of two by saying, 'Home', whenever they were within a mile of their house, showing that she recognized familiar landmarks. She memorized the names of letters as a two year old and can now identify a few familiar words such as her name, her mother's name and some names of shops that she visits regularly. Of course, there is a balance of nurture and nature at work here: Carrie is naturally a strong visual learner, but her mother also supplied the environment within which Carrie could utilize this natural ability.

Practitioners now know that young children learn best within a play and exploratory type of environment, rather than from a formal 'instruction' model where the focus is placed upon the 'The Three Rs'. However, it is important to introduce concepts such as letter and number recognition into everyday play activities. Carrie's mother did not actively 'teach' Carrie to recognize the alphabet, but she did give Carrie a wide variety of experience with print, such as looking through junk mail and picking out the letters from her name, or pretending to 'read' cooking instructions. The result was that Carrie learned to identify letters and numbers at an early age. Research shows that there is a correlation between children who can identify letters before entering school and later attainment in literacy. A review into the implementation of the National Literacy Strategy in reception classes gives a wealth of information about early literacy learning:

> There are also strong links between children's 'orthographic' development on entry to school and their subsequent progress. Children's ability to write their name without a model has been found to be correlated with a number of aspects of writing at seven years (Blatchford, 1991). In addition, there is a strong link between children's early letter-name knowledge and their subsequent reading development (Blatchford et al., 1987; Blatchford and Plewis, 1990). However, the results on later attainment from the direct teaching of letter names have been largely inconclusive (Riley, 1996).

The Standards Site, DfES[74]

It is important not to confuse this sort of stimulating, enriching activity with inappropriate formal instruction. The NLS review goes on to point out that:

Teachers have to strike a balance between promoting early progress and avoiding an inappropriate emphasis on academic provision for children so young.

Strong visual learners tend to visualize situations before they engage in activity. They sometimes 'rehearse' a game in their mind, for example, picturing what will be the outcome of a session in the home corner. They recognize patterns easily and can reproduce them accurately. They often repeat a previous experience by visualizing it first, for example by arranging the small world toys in the same way as the day before in order to continue a previous game. They respond to visual prompts during circle or story time. They tend to remember experiences visually, and respond to photographs or pictures more readily than to lengthy discussions. Visual learners pay attention to detail in books, and remember visual details about experiences that others find hard to recall, such as the clothes that somebody wore or the pattern that the snacks made as they were laid out on a tray. They easily memorize the tags and labels around the classroom and can identify other children's labels in addition to their own. These children usually grow up to learn to read whole words, often before gaining full phonetic understanding, and find learning to spell easy.

You can appeal to the visual learners in your setting by presenting information visually, encouraging children to picture what they are going to do before they begin an activity, and using language such as, 'How will the tractor look when it is finished?' or, 'Can you imagine what will happen when we take this to the office?' By working in this way, you will also help the auditory and kinesthetic learners develop their skills in visual learning.

Auditory learning

 If any type of prenatal stimulation is going to make a difference to a baby's mental development, it is auditory input.

Lise Eliot [75]

In contrast to vision, hearing develops early but matures slowly. The neural structures for hearing begin functioning well before birth, but are not fully matured until the child reaches school age. We know that babies at birth can often recognize familiar sounds and that they know their mother's voice almost immediately. We also know that the more high-quality language children hear, the stronger their auditory and verbal development will be.

Samantha's greatest strength is in auditory learning. She enjoys story-telling sessions in the car with her mum and dad, and does not need pictures as an aid to concentration. When she goes to the supermarket with her mum she tends to maintain a running commentary as they shop.

Samantha is drawing upon her memory of a visit to Uncle Mark's house, triggered by her mother mentioning that they needed to go to the fish counter first. Whereas a visual learner might be picturing the memory, Samantha is talking it through, and needs her mother to help her to connect all her ideas successfully. Although her mother simply 'ums and ahs' through this conversation, she later brings up the subject in the car and helps Samantha to make sense of her memory.

Auditory learners have good listening skills and enjoy group story-telling, circle time and music sessions. They like to hear explanations and will often seek out an adult to talk to. They listen to answers and respond well to verbal feedback about their activities. They learn through language, and often engage in internal dialogue as they process their understanding. Pole-bridging often comes naturally to young auditory learners. If an adult joins in to provide verbal feedback and asks the right types of questions, she is maximizing the experience for the child with an auditory learning preference.

Auditory learners often like to engage in experimentation with language and word-play. They benefit from talking through an experience or activity, or listening to somebody else's description. Using language such as, 'Tell me about your picture,' suits auditory learners, along with specific comments about what they are doing, such as, 'You've wound the string around the box and pulled it tight. Can you tell me what might happen when you cut it?' Plenary sessions are particularly important to auditory learners. Of course, this will also benefit the visual and kinesthetic learners.

Kinesthetic learning

'My dad says that I'm unstoppable on the climbing frame.

Myra, aged four'

Research has shown that exercise and physical movement is not just healthy for the body: it is good for the brain too. Yet the ability to learn through physical activity is often seen as being 'inferior' to learning visually or aurally. Howard Gardner challenges this perception by including 'Bodily-kinesthetic' in his list of multiple intelligences.[76] He argues that a kinesthetic intelligence is as valid as a mathematical or linguistic intelligence.

Read about the multiple intelligences on page 122.

Kishan is a strongly kinesthetic learner. He was an early walker and learned to climb onto the kitchen counter by the age of fourteen months. From a very young age, Kishan always wanted to hold objects to explore them. He thrives outdoors where he can work with the big blocks, ropes and tyres, and he is often found out there working as chief engineer! Kishan can visualize how a construction will take shape and is good at manoeuvring the equipment through three dimensions.

Kishan is very agile and climbs confidently on the most challenging apparatus. He enjoys setting out different arrangements with the climbing frames. He likes the dramatic aspects of stories, and loves to get up and do actions and move during story times. He often makes up actions to go with songs and rhymes. When his teacher describes a task, she often notices that Kishan is doing the actions that will accompany the activity. This is not conscious on Kishan's part: he needs to move in order to internalize information. He enjoys activities such as 'Body Maths', where the children actively represent mathematical concepts with their bodies.

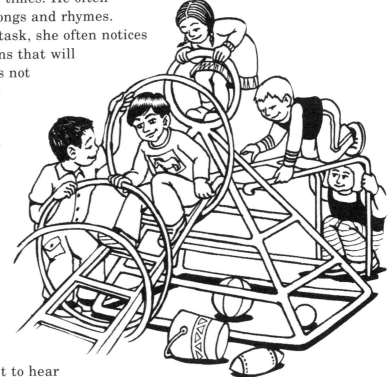

Kinesthetic learners learn best through physical activity. They can present their parents with challenges in managing their behaviour – preferring to stand on the sofa than to sit to hear a story! They are well co-ordinated and are usually eager to improve their physical performance. This often leads to a competitive nature, where they enjoy climbing the highest apparatus, or riding the bikes the fastest or down the steepest slope. They demonstrate greater dexterity than their peers and have a strong sense of timing.

Kinesthetic learners often choose to play outdoors. The challenge for practitioners is to find ways to bring kinesthetic learning indoors, such as providing easels with marker pens for writing, large comfortable mats for small world play and plenty of space in the book corner. These children find listening to stories easier if there are frequent breaks for movement or to shift position. Kinesthetic learners benefit from being encouraged to do actions to accompany a story. In music sessions they like to play instruments or clap or dance along to the music. This helps them to process the experience more fully. These children often need to be given a lot of help to develop the skills of 'good sitting' and 'good listening'. Breaking up sessions with brain breaks – short periods of physical activity – helps them to maintain their focus and develop their visual and auditory skills without feeling frustrated or losing concentration due to unrealistic expectations being made of them.

Now that we have recognized and provided for the three ways of learning, we can move on to consider a more sophisticated model for understanding intelligence – that of the multiple intelligences.

Step 4: Engaging the multiple intelligences

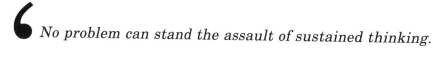

No problem can stand the assault of sustained thinking.

Voltaire [77]

I was proposing an expansion of the term 'intelligence' so that it would encompass many capacities that had been considered outside its scope.

Howard Gardner [78]

There are many theories about the nature of intelligence, with the most commonly understood and accepted being that of IQ. The problem with the IQ model is that it assumes that intelligence is a fixed phenomena that is measurable through one test. It does not allow for the concept that intelligence can be increased through experience, nor does it allow for the idea that each individual possesses different types of intelligence. Howard Gardner offers a different model: that of the multiple intelligences.

The potential for bias in intelligence testing, combined with the idea that intelligence is something that one is born with (nature) and only somewhat influenced by the environment (nurture), makes the theory of 'multiple intelligences' a much more satisfactory model. The eight 'intelligences' are:

 Linguistic

 Logical-mathematical

 Musical

 Bodily-kinesthetic

 Spatial

 Interpersonal

 Intrapersonal

 Naturalist

The first two intelligences in the list are the ones that are most valued by our society and education system. If you are good with languages or are a logical-mathematical thinker, you are likely to succeed in our culture. Yet who could deny that Mozart or Bach or John Lennon were 'intelligent'? Or any of the world's great athletes, or artists, or diplomats, psychiatrists or biologists? When you move away from the limited thinking of intelligence being easily measurable and tested, and see the range of intelligences that exist in Gardner's list, the potential for valuing each child's potential increases dramatically.

The linguistic child

A child with a strong linguistic intelligence will have an intuitive feel for language. He will usually speak early and his language will develop fast. He will have a good memory for new vocabulary and will make connections between words, for example realizing that 'desert' and 'dessert' sound similar but have very different meanings. He will experiment with sounds and rhymes and enjoy games like making up nonsense words. The linguistic child will usually show a keen interest in the written word, and will enjoy stories and story-telling. He will learn the words to nursery rhymes and songs easily. He will pole-bridge naturally and uninhibitedly and will contribute to discussions enthusiastically.

The logical-mathematical child

A child with a strong logical-mathematical intelligence will exhibit a strong memory for patterns and links. She will have an intuitive feel for what is orderly. She will often create patterns in her play, such as lining up the toy cars in order of size, colour or shape. She will notice when a pattern is broken. She will make links between ideas and experiences: if there were ten beads in one pot, how many will fit in this similar pot? She will automatically estimate and experiment. Problems will intrigue and excite her, and she will problem solve enthusiastically. Her play will be organized and focused, and she will apply her mathematical understanding from one situation to another.

The musical child

A child with a strong musical intelligence will learn melodies easily and will be able to copy patterns. She will develop a good sense of pitch and rhythm at a young age. She will copy actions and techniques in music sessions and will often use her whole body when she responds to music. If given the opportunity, she will develop good technical musical skills, but even if she does not have this opportunity, she will have a natural 'feel' for music that cannot easily be taught. She will enjoy composing music and will hear 'tones in her head'. She will be uninhibited about singing and making music either spontaneously or in more formal group sessions.

The bodily-kinesthetic child

A child with a strong bodily-kinesthetic intelligence will develop good motor skills at an early age. He will have an awareness of his body and its place in space. He will learn through physical activity and will be good at Brain Gym®. He will have a good sense of timing and be able to create and repeat sequences of movement. His movements will often be precise and he will take pleasure in repeating a movement and improving on it. He will often be a good mimic and be able to imitate other people's actions accurately. He will take pleasure in using tools and manipulating toys.

The spatial child

A child with a strong spatial intelligence will be able to re-create scenes after the event, for example making the same layout with the small world toys the day after a complex game. She will be good at memory games. She will be able to visualize objects being rotated through three dimensions, for example, when building junk models in the technology area. She will have a good concept of the layout of a room and will often be able to re-create a journey and recognize landmarks. She will usually have a good sense of colour and will be experimental in her artwork.

The interpersonal child

A child with a strong interpersonal intelligence will play collaboratively at a young age. He will also develop a strong sense of empathy, often noticing other children if they are showing distress, displaying signs of distress himself in response. He will alter his behaviour according to that of others and show sensitivity to moods. He will respond to books and stories about personalities and emotional issues. He will be anxious to have friends and will usually choose to work with others. He will enjoy tasks that demand a team approach and will usually be able to take turns and see other children's points of view.

The intrapersonal child

The interpersonal and intrapersonal intelligences often go hand-in-hand. A child with a strong intrapersonal intelligence will therefore often display many of the characteristics of the interpersonal child. He will develop a sense of self earlier than many of his peers. He will be able to talk about his own emotions, and will generally be good at recognizing those of others. He will talk readily about how he feels and will often have a very strong sense of justice, causing him to sometimes seem intractable. He will respond thoughtfully to stories about dilemmas and feelings, and will want to relate fiction to his own personal experiences.

The naturalist child

A child with a strong naturalist intelligence will enjoy being outdoors, especially in the garden, grassed or wild area. She will notice details about the natural world and will be enthusiastic about any activity that involves animals, plants or insects. She will categorize things and notice patterns and relationships. She will enjoy taking responsibility for plants or pets, and will show concern for the environment. She will enjoy looking at books about the natural world and may develop a deep knowledge about one or more aspects of wildlife.

Gardner's theory is that each individual person has an individual combination of these different intelligences. Each child has a combination of different intelligences in different strengths, and the environment will then influence how these different intelligences develop and flourish. It would be unnecessary and somewhat ridiculous to attempt to assess children against each of the eight intelligences. However, it is a valuable exercise to think about which intelligences are a particular strength or weakness for each child. This can be done very quickly and easily, by making a list of the children, and drawing columns down the side, one for each of the intelligences. You can then write S in the grid for 'strength' and W for 'weakness'. Some practitioners ask parents to fill in a similar profile for their child, which gives an alternative perspective. It is interesting to also assess your own multiple intelligence profile, as your individual preferences will influence how you teach.

A simple way to make sure that your curriculum is balanced is to add a checklist with eight boxes to your planning sheet. Just tick each box when a planned activity fosters that particular intelligence. You should then be able to see if any particular intelligence is being over- or under-emphasized in your setting. Once you have done this and have decided that Vishal is musically intelligent or that James has great interpersonal skills, or that Gill and Peta need help with developing their linguistic intelligence, you can be creative in planning ways to work with each unique child.

The effect of a curriculum that caters for the multiple intelligences is far-reaching. Children's individual learning styles and needs are catered for, and the curriculum becomes increasingly child-centred. Once the curriculum really matches the child's needs, he can be truly successful and his self-esteem flourishes. With increased self-esteem, his motivation to learn increases. We have provided an environment where practitioners teach for intelligence, and children learn with intelligence.

Some points for reflection:

How flexible is your planning and your timetable, and how does it allow for you to be spontaneous and creative? How do you follow up on children's interests and extend their learning? Which of the ideas might you wish to try out?

How well do the children in your setting co-operate in pairs or groups? How much opportunity do they get for group work? How do you ensure that they learn the skills that are necessary for success in a group?

Can you identify which children in your setting are strongly visual, auditory or kinesthetic learners? What learning style do you personally prefer? How do you cater for the different types of learners in your setting and how do you help children to develop all three styles regardless of their preference?

Which of the multiple intelligences is your greatest strength? Do you value all eight intelligences equally? Is it clear to the children that you do so? Can you identify the multiple intelligence strengths of the children in your care? How do you cater for their individual learning needs?

Part Four

Now that you have reached the end of this book, you have completed the first part of the brain-based journey. But the learning is only just beginning! When you put into practice the techniques that you have read about here, you will discover even more about the child's brain and learning.

Hopefully you now feel enthusiastic about beginning to put these ideas into practice in your setting. Do this at your own pace and in the order that makes most sense to you – there is no right or wrong way to introduce brain-based learning into any setting. After a time, you will look back and feel inspired by what you and the children in your care have learned and achieved.

Learning is a lifelong journey, full of excitement and adventure. May the journey be both rewarding and enjoyable, and may you and the children in your care have every success along the way!

Website information

www.acceleratedlearning.co.uk

Nicola Call's website. Nicola's website gives explanations of the theory behind brain-based learning along with practical information, such as lists of useful music, suggestions for brain break activities, and reading lists for those working in the Early Years and Key Stages 1 and 2. Up-to-date information is posted about brain-based publications, resources and staff training.

www.featherstone.uk.com

Sally Featherstone's website. Sally's website contains information about the publications from Featherstone Education Ltd, and many other Early Years books for practitioners. The site also contains articles and newsletters for practitioners on aspects of particular interest to those working with the Foundation Stage.

Bibliography

Abbott, Lesley and Nutbrown, Cathy (eds), *Experiencing Reggio Emilia*. Open University Press, 2001

Ballinger, Erich, *The Learning Gym*. Edu-Kinesthetics, 1996

Basic Skills Agency, *Securing Boys' Literacy*. Basic Skills Agency, Tel 0870 600 2400

Biddulph, Steve, *The Secret of Happy Children*, Thorsons; HarperCollins Publishers, 1998

Bilton, Helen, *Outdoor Play in the Early Years*. David Fulton, 1998

Boyd Cadwell, Louise, *Bringing Reggio Emilia Home*. Teacher's College Press, 1997

Brewer, Chris and Campbell, Don, *Rhythms of Learning*. Zephyr, 1991

Bruce, Tina, *Learning through Play: Babies, Toddlers and the Foundation Years*. Hodder Stoughton, 2001

Buzan, Tony with Buzan, Barry, *The Mind Map Book – How to Use Radiant Thinking to Maximise Your Brain's Untapped Potential*. Penguin Books, 1993

Campbell, Don, *The Mozart Effect: Tapping the Power of Music to Heal the Body, Strengthen the Mind, and Unlock the Creative Spirit*. HarperCollins Publishers Inc, 1997

Campbell, Don, *The Mozart Effect for Children: Awakening Your Child's Mind, Health, and Creativity with Music*. HarperCollins Publishers, Inc, 2000

Ceppi & Zini, *Children, Spaces, Relationships – Metaproject for An Environment for Young Children*. Reggio Children, 1999

Cousins, Jacqui, *Listening to Four Year Olds*. National Early Years Network, 1999

Dennison Paul E. Gail E., *Brain Gym*. Edu-Kinesthetics, 1989

Donaldson, Margaret, *Children's Minds*. WW Norton and Company, 1979

Eliot, Lise, *What's going on in There? How the Brain and Mind Develop in the First Five Years of Life*. Bantam Books, 2000

Gardner, Howard, *Frames of Mind – The Theory of Multiple Intelligences*. Basic Books, 1993

Gardner, Howard, *Intelligence Reframed – Multiple Intelligences for the 21st Century*. Basic Books, 1999

Goer, Henci, *The Thinking Woman's Guide to a Better Birth*. The Berkley Publishing Group, 1999

Goleman, Daniel, *Emotional Intelligence. Why it Can Matter More than IQ*. Bloomsbury Publishing Plc, 1995

Gottman, John, *The Heart of Parenting*. Bloomsbury, 1997

Greenman, Jim, *Caring Spaces, Learning Places: Children's Environments That Work*. Exchange Press, 1988

Greenspan, Stanley, *Building Healthy Minds: The Six Experiences that Create Intelligence and Emotional Growth in Babies and Young Children*. Perseus Publishing, 1999

Hannaford Carla, *Smart Moves: Why Learning is not all in your Head*. Great Ocean Publishers, 1995

Hart, Betty and Risley, Todd, *Meaningful Differences in the Everyday Experience of Young American Children*. Paul H Brookes Pub Co, 1995

Harter, Susan, 'Teacher and classmate influences on scholastic motivation, self-esteem, and level of voice in adolescents', in J. Juvonen and K. R. Wentzel (eds), *Social Motivation, Understanding Children's School Adjustment*. Cambridge University Press, 1996

Healy, Jane M., *Endangered Minds – Why Children Don't Think – and What We Can Do About It*. Touchstone Books, Simon & Schuster, 1990

Healy, Jane, *Failure to Connect: How Computers Affect our Children's Minds – for Better and Worse*. Simon Schuster, 1998

Hendrick, Joanne, *The Whole Child*. Prentice-Hall Inc, 1996

Howe, Christine, *Gender and Classroom Interaction: A Research Review*. The Scottish Council for Research in Education, 1997

Jensen, Eric, *Teaching with the Brain in Mind*. ASDC (USA), 1998

Kohn, Alfie, *Punished by Rewards: The Trouble with Gold Stars, Incentive Plans, As, Praise and Other Bribes*. Houghton Mifflin Company, New York, 1993

Kotulak, Ronald, *Inside the Brain: Revolutionary Discoveries of How The Mind Works*. Andrews McMeel Publishing, 1997

Miles, Elizabeth, *Tune Your Brain: Using Music to Manage Your Mind, Body and Mood*. Berkley Publishing Group, 1997

Miller, Judy, *Never too Young – How Young Children Can Take Responsibility and Make Decisions*. National Early Years Network, 1996

Mosley, Jenny, *Quality Circle Time in the Primary Classroom*. LDA, 1999

Nutbrown, Cathy, *Threads of Thinking*. Paul Chapman,1999

Ouvry, Marjorie, *Exercising Muscles and Minds*. National Early Years Network, 2000

Pascal Chris and Bertram Tony, *Effective Early Learning* (Case Studies in Improvement). Hodder & Stoughton, 1997

Reggio Children, *The Hundred Languages of Children*. Reggio Children, 1996

Roehlkepartain and Leffert, *What Children Need to Succeed*. Free Spirit, EY Network, 1996

Schiller, Pam, *Start Smart! Building Brain Power in the Early Years*. Gryphon House, Inc, 1999

Sears, William, and Sears, Martha, RN, *The Baby Book*: *Everything You Need to Know About Your Baby from Birth to Age Two*. Little, Brown and Company, 1993

Tizard, Barbara and Hughes, Martin, *Young Children Learning*. Harvard University Press, 1984

The Thinking Child

References

1 Kotulak, Ronald, *Inside the Brain: Revolutionary Discoveries of How the Mind Works*. Andrews McMeel Publishing, 1997

2 Miles, Elizabeth, *Tune Your Brain: Using Music to Manage Your Mind, Body and Mood*. Berkley Publishing Group, 1997

3 Goodwin, Frederick, quoted by Kotulak, Ronald, *Inside the Brain: Revolutionary Discoveries of How the Mind Works*. Andrews McMeel Publishing, 1997

4 Montessori, Maria, *The Absorbent Mind*. Henry Holt, 1995

5 Richards, M., et al., Birth Weight and Cognitive Function in the British 1946 Birth Cohort: Longitudinal Population Based Study. British Medical Journal, Jan. 27, 2001

6 Darwin, Charles, *Chapter 2 – On the Manner of Development of Man from Some Lower Form. The Descent of Man*. Prometheus Books (reprint edition), 1997

7 Research quoted by Kotulak, Ronald. Paper presented in Chicago to the conference 'Brain Development in Young Children: New Frontiers for Research, Policy and Practice'. 13 June 1996

8 Sears, William, and Sears, Martha, *The Baby Book: Everything You Need to Know About Your Baby from Birth to Age Two*. Little, Brown and Company, 1993

9 Biddulph, Steve, *The Secret of Happy Children*. Thorsons; HarperCollins Publishers, 1998

10 Dennison, Paul. E. and Gail, E., *Brain Gym*. Edu-Kinesthetics, 1989; www.braingym.org

11 Work of Gage, Fred H. (Salk Institute, California) and Eriksson, Peter S. (Göteborg University, Sweden). *The Scientific American*, November 1998

12 Anderson, James W. *The American Journal of Clinical Nutrition*, October 1999

13 Peal, Elizabeth and Lambert, Wallace, *The Relation of Bilingualism to Intelligence*. Psychological Monographs, Vol. 76; Lambert, Wallace, *Effects of Bilingualism on the Individual: Cognitive and Socio-cultural Consequences*, quoted in Hornby, P.A., *Bilingualism: Psychological, Social and Educational Implications*. Academic Press, 1974

14 Penn State Children's Hospital, Reuters. Quoted at www.cosmiverse.com

15 Research by Sapolsky, Robert, quoted in Kotulak, Ronald, *Inside the Brain: Revolutionary Discoveries of How the Mind Works*. Andrews McMeel Publishing, 1997

16 Department of Health, *Our Healthier Nation: A Contract for Health*. Green Paper, 1998

17 Pollitt, E. 'Annual Review of Nutrition', *Iron Deficiency and Cognitive Function*. Vol. 13: 521–37, 1993

18 James, J. A. and Laing, G. J., *Iron Deficiency Anemia*. Current Pediatrics, 1994

19 Research by Scholey, Andrew et al. (University of Northumbria and the Cognitive Research Unit), Reading presented to a symposium at the British Psychological Society's annual conference in Blackpool, 13 March 2002; www.uk.news.yahoo.com

20 Lavigne, John V. et al., *Journal of Developmental and Behavioral Pediatrics*, June 2000

21 Coe, C. L., Glass, J. C., Wiener, S. G., Levine, S., 'Behavioral, but not Physiological: Adaptation to Repeated Separation in Mother and Infant Primates', *Psychoneuroendocrinology*, 8(4): 401–409, 1983. Cited in API News, Vol. 5, No. 1, 2002

22 Goleman, Daniel, *Emotional Intelligence: Why It Can Matter More than IQ*. Bloomsbury Publishing, 1995

23 Lepper, M. R. and Hodell, M., 'Intrinsic Motivation in the Classroom', In: Ames, R. and Ames, C. (eds), *Research on Motivation in Education (Vol. 3): Goals and Cognitions*. Academic Press, 1989

24 Goleman, Daniel, *Emotional Intelligence: Why It Can Matter More than IQ*. Bloomsbury Publishing Plc, 1995

25 Bornstein and Tamis-LeMonda, *Day Care and Early Education*. 1994

26 Mosley, Jenny, *Quality Circle Time in the Primary Classroom*. LDA, 1999

27 Hannaford, Carla, *Smart Moves: Why Learning is not all in Your Head*. Great Ocean Publishers, 1995

28 Montessori, Maria, 1870–1952, Italian physician, author and educational pioneer; Gettman, David, *Basic Montessori: Learning Activities for Under Fives*. ABC-Clio Ltd, 1987

29 Howe, Christine, *Gender and Classroom Interaction: A Research Review*. The Scottish Council for Research in Education, 1997

30 Kohn, Alfie, *Punished by Rewards: The Trouble with Gold Stars, Incentive Plans, As, Praise and Other Bribes*. Houghton Mifflin Company New York, 1993

31 Hendrick, Joanne, *The Whole Child*. Prentice-Hall Inc, 1996

32 Cadbury Heath Primary School, Bristol. Case study quoted at www.standards.dfee.gov.uk

33 Ghazvini, A. S. and Readdick, C. A., *Parent-Caregiver Communication and Quality of Care in Diverse Child Care Settings*, quoted in Hendrick, Joanne, *The Whole Child*. Prentice-Hall Inc, 1996

34 *Bullock Report*, DES, 1975; Brooks, Gormon, et al., quoted at The Standards Website, DfES, 1976, www.standards.dfes.gov.uk

35 Clarke, John Henrik, 'A Search for Identity', *Social Casework*, Vol. 51, No. 5: 259–264, May 1970

36 Kotulak, Ronald, Inside the *Brain: Revolutionary Discoveries of How the Mind Works*. Andrews McMeel Publishing, 1997

37 Castellanos, F. Xavier, MD et al., research presented in *Archives of General Psychiatry*, July 1996

38 BBCs *Panorama*. Broadcast 10 April 2000

39 *The Observer*, Sunday 9 September 2001. Quoted at www.guardian.co.uk

40 National Deaf Children's Society statistics; www.ndcs.org.uk

41 Mrs S. James, reception teacher, Seer Green Church of England Combined School, Buckinghamshire

42 Kohn, Alfie, *Punished by Rewards: The Trouble with Gold Stars, Incentive Plans, As, Praise and Other Bribes*. Houghton Mifflin Company New York, 1993

43 *Guidance on the Organisation of the National Literacy Strategy in Reception Classes.* DfEE, 0153/2000, September 2000

44 *Guidance on the Organisation of the Daily Mathematics Lesson in Reception Classes.* DfEE, 0088/2000, May 2000

45 Hart, Betty and Risley, Todd, *Meaningful Differences in the Everyday Experience of Young American Children.* Paul H Brookes Pub Co, 1995

46 Quotation from University of Kansas; Office of University Relations website at www.ur.ku.edu

47 Qualifications and Curriculum Authority, *Can do better: Raising boys' achievement in English.* 1998

48 Buzan, Tony with Buzan, Barry, *The Mind Map Book: How to Use Radiant Thinking to Maximise Your Brain's Untapped Potential.* Penguin Books, 1993

49 Einstein, Albert, 1879–1955, German-born American physicist, author and Nobel Laureate

50 *Curriculum Guidance for the Foundation Stage.* DfEE, May 2000

51 Berg, C. L. van den, Hol, T., Everts, H., Koolhaas, J. M., van Ree, J. M., Spruijt, B. M., 'Play is Indispensable for an Adequate Development of Coping with Social Challenges in the Rat', *Developmental Psychobiology,* 34: 129–138, 1999

52 Greenspan, Stanley, MD, *Building Healthy Minds: The Six Experiences that Create Intelligence and Emotional Growth in Babies and Young Children.* Perseus Publishing, 1999

53 *Curriculum Guidance for the Foundation Stage.* DfEE, May 2000

54 Cousins, Jacqui, *Listening to Four Year Olds.* National Early Years Network, 1999

55 Bruce, Tina, *Learning through Play: Babies, Toddlers and the Foundation Years.* Hodder and Stoughton, 2001

56 Campbell, Don, *The Mozart Effect for Children: Awakening Your Child's Mind, Health, and Creativity with Music.* HarperCollins Publishers Inc, 2000

57 Hurwitz, I., Wolff, P. H. Bortnick, B. D. and Kokas, K., *Nonmusical Effects of the Kodaly Music Curriculum in Primary Grade Children.* MuSICA Research Notes, Vol. 1, Issue 2, *Journal of Learning Disabilities,* 8: 45–51, 1975. www.musica.uci.edu

58 *Education Week,* 12 March 1997; www.edweek.org

59 Campbell, Don, *The Mozart Effect: Tapping the Power of Music to Heal the Body, Strengthen the Mind, and Unlock the Creative Spirit.* HarperCollins Publishers Inc, 1997

60 *The National Literacy Strategy: Review of Research and other Related Evidence.* www.standards.dfee.gov.uk

61 Research quoted in Campbell, Don, *The Mozart Effect: Tapping the Power of Music to Heal the Body, Strengthen the Mind, and Unlock the Creative Spirit.* HarperCollins Publishers Inc, 1997

62 Hannaford, Carla, *Smart Moves: Why Learning is not all in Your Head.* Great Ocean Publishers, 1995

63 Hannaford, Carla, *Smart Moves: Why Learning is not all in Your Head.* Great Ocean Publishers, 1995

64 Prime Minister Tony Blair's speech regarding the launch of a 50 million computer scheme, at Greensward College, Essex, December 2001, reported in *The Guardian*, online, 10 December 2001

65 Healy, Jane, *Failure to Connect: How Computers Affect our Children's Minds – for Better and Worse*. Simon Schuster, 1998

66 Research quoted in Howe, Christine, *Gender and Classroom Interaction: A Research Review*. The Scottish Council for Research in Education, 1997

67 Howe, Christine, *Gender and Classroom Interaction: A Research Review*. The Scottish Council for Research in Education, 1997

68 Research quoted in Kotulak, Ronald, *Inside the Brain: Revolutionary Discoveries of How the Mind Works*. Andrews McMeel Publishing, 1997

69 Einstein, Albert, 1879–1955, German-born American physicist, author and Nobel Laureate

70 Holmes, Oliver Wendell, 1809–1894, American physician, professor and author

71 Watson, Judith, 'Working in Groups: Social and Cognitive Effects in a Special Class', *British Journal of Special Education*, Vol. 26, No. 2, 87-95(9), June 1999

72 Einstein, Albert, 1879–1955, German-born American physicist, author and Nobel Laureate

73 Eliot, Lise, *What's Going on in There? How the Brain and Mind Develop in the First Five Years of Life*. Bantam Books, p. 209, 1999

74 The Standards Site. DfES; www.standards.dfes.gov.uk

75 Eliot, Lise, *What's Going on in There? How the Brain and Mind Develop in the First Five Years of Life*. Bantam Books, p. 239, 1999

76 Gardner, Howard, *Intelligence Reframed – Multiple Intelligences for the 21st Century*. Basic Books, 1999

77 Voltaire, François Marie Arouet de, 1694–1778, French author and philosopher

78 Gardner, Howard, *Intelligence Reframed – Multiple Intelligences for the 21st Century*. Basic Books, 1999

Other publications

THE SCHOOL EFFECTIVENESS SERIES

Book 1: **Accelerated Learning in the Classroom** by Alistair Smith
ISBN: 1-85539-034-5

Book 2: **Effective Learning Activities** by Chris Dickinson
ISBN: 1855390353

Book 3: **Effective Heads of Department** by Phil Jones & Nick Sparks
ISBN: 1-85539-036-1

Book 4: **Lessons are for Learning** by Mike Hughes
ISBN: 185539-038-8

Book 5: **Effective Learning in Science** by Paul Denley and Keith Bishop
ISBN: 1-85539-039-6

Book 6: **Raising Boys' Achievement** by Jon Pickering
ISBN: 1-85539-040-X

Book 7: **Effective Provision for Able & Talented Children** by Barry Teare
ISBN: 1-85539-041-8

Book 8: **Effective Careers Education & Guidance** by Andrew Edwards
and Anthony Barnes
ISBN: 1-85539-045-0

Book 9: **Best behaviour and Best behaviour FIRST AID** by Peter Relf, Rod Hirst,
Jan Richardson and Georgina Youdell
ISBN: 1-85539-046-9

Best behaviour FIRST AID
ISBN: 1-85539-047-7 (pack of 5 booklets)

Book 10: **The Effective School Governor** by David Marriott
ISBN 1-85539-042-6 (including free audio tape)

Book 11: **Improving Personal Effectiveness for Managers in Schools**
by James Johnson
ISBN 1-85539-049-3

Book 12: **Making Pupil Data Powerful** by Maggie Pringle and Tony Cobb
ISBN 1-85539-052-3

Book 13: **_Closing the Learning Gap_** by Mike Hughes
ISBN 1-85539-051-5

Book 14: **_Getting Started_** by Henry Leibling
ISBN 1-85539-054-X

Book 15: **_Leading the Learning School_** by Colin Weatherley
ISBN 1-85539-070-1

Book 16: **_Adventures in Learning_** by Mike Tilling
ISBN 1-85539-073-6

Book 17: **_Strategies for Closing the Learning Gap_** by Mike Hughes & Andy Vass
ISBN 1-85539-075-2

Book 18: **_Classroom Management_** by Phillip Waterhouse and Chris Dickinson
ISBN 1-85539-079-5

Book 19: **_Effective Teachers_** by Tony Swainston
ISBN 1-85539-125-2

Book 20: **_Transforming Teaching and Learning_** by Colin Weatherley, Bruce Bonney,
John Kerr and Jo Morrison
ISBN 1-85539-080-9

Book 21: **_Effective Teachers in Primary Schools_** by Tony Swainston
ISBN 1-85539-153-8

ACCELERATED LEARNING SERIES

General Editor: Alistair Smith

Accelerated Learning in Practice by Alistair Smith
ISBN 1-85539-048-5

The ALPS Approach: Accelerated Learning in Primary Schools by Alistair Smith
and Nicola Call
ISBN 1-85539-056-6

MapWise by Oliver Caviglioli and Ian Harris
ISBN 1-85539-059-0

The ALPS Approach Resource Book by Alistair Smith and Nicola Call
ISBN 1-85539-078-7

Creating an Accelerated Learning School by Mark Lovatt & Derek Wise
ISBN 1-85539-074-4

ALPS StoryMaker by Stephen Bowkett
ISBN 1-85539-076-0

Thinking for Learning by Mel Rockett & Simon Percival
ISBN 1-85539-096-5

Reaching out to all learners by Cheshire LEA
ISBN 1-85539-143-0

Leading Learning by Alistair Smith
ISBN 1-85539-089-2

Bright Sparks by Alistair Smith
ISBN 1-85539-088-4

Move It by Alistair Smith
ISBN 1-85539-123-6

EDUCATION PERSONNEL MANAGEMENT SERIES

Education Personnel Management handbooks will help headteachers, senior managers and governors to manage a broad range of personnel issues.

The Well Teacher – management strategies for beating stress, promoting staff health and reducing absence by Maureen Cooper
ISBN 1-85539-058-2

Managing Challenging People – dealing with staff conduct by Bev Curtis and Maureen Cooper
ISBN 1-85539-057-4

Managing Poor Performance – handling staff capability issues by Bev Curtis and Maureen Cooper
ISBN 1-85539-062-0

Managing Allegations Against Staff – personnel and child protection issues in schools by Maureen Cooper & Bev Curtis
ISBN 1-85539-072-8

Managing Recruitment and Selection – appointing the best staff by Maureen Cooper & Bev Curtis
ISBN 1-85539-077-9

Managing Redundancies – dealing with reduction and reorganisation of staff by Maureen Cooper & Bev Curtis
ISBN 1-85539-082-5

Managing Pay in Schools – performance management and pay in schools by Bev Curtis
ISBN 1-85539-087-6

VISIONS OF EDUCATION SERIES

The Unfinished Revolution by John Abbott and Terry Ryan
ISBN 1-85539-064-7

The Learning Revolution by Jeannette Vos & Gordon Dryden
ISBN 1-85539-085-X

Wise Up by Guy Claxton
ISBN 1-85539-099-X

ABLE & TALENTED CHILDREN COLLECTION

Effective Resources for Able and Talented Children by Barry Teare
ISBN 1-85539-050-7

More Effective Resources for Able and Talented Children by Barry Teare
ISBN 1-85539-063-9

Challenging Resources for Able and Talented Children by Barry Teare
ISBN 1-85539-122-8

MODEL LEARNING

Thinking Skills & Eye Q by Oliver Caviglioli, Ian Harris & Bill Tindall
ISBN 1-85539-091-4

Class Maps by Oliver Caviglioli & Ian Harris
ISBN 1-85539-139-2

OTHER TITLES FROM NEP

StoryMaker Catch Pack by Stephen Bowkett
ISBN 1-85539-109-0

Becoming Emotionally Intelligent by Catherine Corrie
ISBN 1-85539-069-8

That's Science by Tim Harding
ISBN 1-85539-170-8

The Brain's Behind It by Alistair Smith
ISBN 1-85539-083-3

Help Your Child To Succeed by Bill Lucas & Alistair Smith
ISBN 1-85539-111-2

Tweak to Transform by Mike Hughes
ISBN 1-85539-140-6

Brain Friendly Revision by UFA National Team
ISBN 1-85539-127-9

Numeracy Activities Key Stage 2 by Afzal Ahmed & Honor Williams
ISBN 1-85539-102-3

Numeracy Activities Key Stage 3 by Afzal Ahmed, Honor Williams &
George Wickham
ISBN 1-85539-103-1

Teaching Pupils How to Learn by Bill Lucas, Toby Greany, Jill Rodd & Ray Wicks
ISBN 1-85539-098-1

Basics for School Governors by Joan Sallis
ISBN 1-85539-012-4

Imagine That... by Stephen Bowkett
ISBN 1-85539-043-4

Self-Intelligence by Stephen Bowkett
ISBN 1-85539-055-8

Class Talk by Rosemary Sage
ISBN 1-85539-061-2

Index

The Thinking Child

Brain-based learning for the foundation stage